DIMETOS
and
TWO
EARLY PLAYS

DIMETOS
and
TWO
EARLY PLAYS

ATHOL FUGARD

OXFORD   LONDON   MELBOURNE
OXFORD UNIVERSITY PRESS
1977

Oxford University Press, Walton Street, Oxford OX2 6DP

OXFORD   LONDON   GLASGOW   NEW YORK
TORONTO   MELBOURNE   WELLINGTON   CAPE TOWN
IBADAN   NAIROBI   DAR ES SALAAM   LUSAKA   KUALA LUMPUR
SINGAPORE   JAKARTA   HONG KONG   TOKYO   DELHI
BOMBAY   CALCUTTA   MADRAS   KARACHI

Casebound edition ISBN 0 19 211390 9
Paperback edition ISBN 0 19 281210 6
(issued simultaneously by Oxford University Press, Oxford, 1977)

Fugard, Athol
   Dimetos; and, Two early plays.
   I. Title
   822   PR9369.F78

   ISBN 0-19-211390-9
   ISBN 0-19-281210-6 Pbk

*Filmset and printed in Great Britain by
Thomson Litho Ltd., East Kilbride, Scotland.*

Contents

DIMETOS

FOR LISA

Act I—In a remote province
Act II—Beside the ocean

CHARACTERS

DIMETOS   an engineer
LYDIA   his orphaned niece
SOPHIA   his housekeeper
DANILO   a young man from the city

This play was commissioned by the Edinburgh Festival and was given its first performance in Edinburgh on 27 August 1975 with the following cast directed by Athol Fugard:

Dimetos	*Carel Trichard*
Lydia	*Vanessa Cooke*
Sophia	*Yvonne Bryceland*
Danilo	*Wilson Dunster*

In 1976 it was produced in a modified version (printed here) in Nottingham and London with the following cast, again directed by the author:

Dimetos	*Paul Scofield*
Lydia	*Celia Quicke*
Sophia	*Yvonne Bryceland*
Danilo	*Ben Kingsley*

ACT ONE

Scene 1

Lydia *is lowered to the bottom of a well to tie ropes round a horse that has fallen down it.*

LYDIA (*calling up*). I'm on his back, Dimetos! What must I do?

DIMETOS'S VOICE. How is he?

LYDIA. Frightened.

VOICE. Keep calm. Make sure you are comfortable.

LYDIA. I am.

VOICE. The two slings . . . can you hear me clearly?

LYDIA. Yes.

VOICE. The first one, as I explained up here, behind his front legs . . . knotted above the withers . . .

[*She follows the instructions. Lying prostrate on the horse's back she slowly positions the first sling. It is very dark; she works by touch, making comforting noises all the time.*]

Take your time. Shout when you are ready.

LYDIA. Ready.

VOICE. The second one . . . in front of his hindquarters, around his flanks . . . take your time. [*She positions the second sling.*]

LYDIA. Ready.

VOICE. Now the ropes around you . . . untie one but don't let it go . . . only one. Give a hard pull when it's free.

[*Straddling the horse she unties one of the ropes around her waist and gives it a hard pull.*]

Right . . . now listen carefully . . . you have got to tie the knot I showed you. I can't see your hands clearly enough to stop you if you make a mistake . . . so listen carefully. Thread a good length through the two rings.

LYDIA. Ready.

VOICE. Take the loose end . . . loop it twice around the other . . . now take it under itself . . . loop it around the other end again . . . and

5

again under itself. Now tighten it. Does it slip?

LYDIA. No.

VOICE. The second sling . . . untie the second rope . . . the same knot . .
listen carefully again . . . the loose end through the two rings . .
[*She repeats the knot.*] Do you want to rest?

LYDIA. No.

VOICE. I am going to slacken the rope you've just tied. Make a loo⟩
the way I showed you and put your foot into it.

LYDIA. Ready.

VOICE. Hold on tight. We are going to pull you up.

Scene 2

Beside a pool. Evening. Dimetos, *unknotting and coiling a lengt⟩
of rope, and* Lydia.

LYDIA. I did it! He's free!

DIMETOS. Come out now, Lydia. Sophia will start worrying if w⟩
are not home soon.
[*Lydia, clean and wet after a swim, dries herself with her dress an⟩
then throws it impulsively into the air.*]

LYDIA. I'm too happy to be shy. And I can't stop laughing! I ca⟩
still see him standing there, his legs shivering while you untie⟩
the ropes and then galloping away . . . No! He walked first, didn'⟩
he? A few steps. And then . . . [*She starts laughing again as sh⟩
relives the horse's moment of liberation.*] He looked so splendid⟩
Why did we have to leave? I could have stayed there and watche⟩
him until it was dark.

DIMETOS. It will certainly be that by the time we get home. Sophi⟩
wouldn't have been too pleased if we'd arrived back with yo⟩
covered from head to foot in mud. Did you get it all out of you⟩
hair?

LYDIA. I'll wash it properly when we get home. I think he was als⟩
laughing. And the way he kept shaking his head as if he couldn⟩
believe it was true. Everybody was laughing! Except you. If ⟩
didn't know you I would have thought you weren't glad that w⟩
had got him out.

DIMETOS. Was it as bad as that?

LYDIA. Yes. But you were, weren't you?

DIMETOS. Of course.

LYDIA. Then why do you do that?

DIMETOS. What?

LYDIA. Hide your feelings.

DIMETOS. There wasn't that much to hide. All I saw galloping away was an obviously stupid animal that we had hauled out of a deep hole. I'm not even sure that he will have learnt a lesson. You must make allowances little one. I've seen more accidents than you. Not all of them had happy endings.

LYDIA. All the more reason for laughing when one does. How do you think it happened?

DIMETOS. At a critical moment he found nothing under hoof and became a helpless victim of that force which attracts masses to each other. He fell in.

LYDIA. Stop joking.

DIMETOS. I'm not. It's a fact ... mysterious! ... but still a fact. 'Every particle of matter in the Universe attracts every other particle with a force whose direction is that of the line joining the two...' It's called Gravity. The potential in all bodies to move or be moved.

LYDIA. I don't want any of your old facts now!

DIMETOS. They're not mine, and they're not old. And what's more you should. They are all that really matter. They'll help you understand a lot more than falling horses little one. That law holds the universe together. But I think I know what you do want. 'Once upon a time there was a horse. He was a very happy horse until the day he noticed that the grass in his field was not as green...'

LYDIA. Don't tease me! I was just wondering how it happened.

DIMETOS. We'll never know. But even if we did it wouldn't have helped us get him out. All I needed was a reasonably accurate estimate of his weight and the breaking strength of theses ropes. I'm an engineer, Lydia, not a story teller. An artisan, not an artist.

LYDIA. Well he has got a story even if you don't care what it is, and you did give it a happy ending.

DIMETOS. That happy ending was made by a system of pulleys with a mechanical advantage of five to one. Anybody who knew how

7

to use them could have done what I did.

LYDIA. But it was *you*. You also don't want people to be grateful to you.

DIMETOS. I don't think that's true.

LYDIA. Oh, yes! When they started to thank you for what you had done, you just turned your back and walked away.

DIMETOS. Their stupidity annoyed me. In any case it was you they should have thanked. Were you frightened?

LYDIA. Yes.

DIMETOS. I wouldn't have let you go down if I wasn't sure I could get you up.

LYDIA. I know that! I meant helping him. It's the first time I've tried to help something that was in real trouble. I was frightened I'd make a mistake.

[*Sitting with her chin on her knees, wide-eyed and clutching her dress. Dimetos takes up an end of the dress and dries her back while she talks.*]

I didn't have time to think about it until you started to lower me. We had been so busy digging, putting up the poles and everything. When I had to take off my dress I just felt shy with all the men staring. I was anxious to go down, to get away from them. But when I stepped off the edge and started to swing... and that one rope got stuck! I thought I'd never reach the bottom. I smelt him first you know. That's when I opened my eyes. It was so terrible finding him down there in the dark... feeling him... living and warm and frightened. I don't ever want to be as frightened as that. I didn't care about anything then, except him, and listening carefully when you started calling down to me.

DIMETOS. You called first.

LYDIA. Did I?

DIMETOS. Yes. 'I'm on his back, Dimetos! What must I do?'

LYDIA [*laughing with embarrassment*]. Uncle.

DIMETOS. No! I liked it. You've earned the right to call me Dimetos now. It was the voice, the demand of a colleague, and equal. Dimetos and Lydia. Come. We must go.

LYDIA [*Singing as she puts on her dress*].
'Over fences and ditches he jumped like a stag,
His silken tail streaming behind like a flag...'

8

[*Dimetos leaves.*]
Hey! Wait for me!

Scene 3

Dimetos's house. A large table with tools. Sophia *and* Danilo.

SOPHIA. He and his niece have gone to help a farmer. A horse has fallen down a well. I don't know when they'll be back.

DANILO. You don't mind if I wait though?

SOPHIA. Of course not.
[*She starts working. Danilo goes to the table.*]

DANILO. This is where he works.

SOPHIA. Yes.
[*Danilo picks up a tool and examines it. He smiles to himself. Sophia looks at him enquiringly.*]

DANILO. On my way here I couldn't help wondering what I would find. None of my guesses were right.

SOPHIA. I'm not sure I understand.

DANILO. I tried to picture this village, his life here.

SOPHIA. I see. We've surprised you, have we?

DANILO. Yes. I didn't expect it to be so isolated, so remote. I'm not just thinking about the day's travelling it took me to get here. That mountain pass puts more than a few miles between you and the rest of the world. Horses at the bottom of wells! Tools that could go into a museum... and Dimetos using them! There's a sense of having travelled back in time. I felt it very strongly when I stopped at a farmhouse to ask the way. The old man treated me with a formal suspicion that made me very conscious of being a stranger.

SOPHIA. They are like that. It took a long time before they accepted us. But once they do they are quite hospitable. You are from the city?

DANILO. Yes.

SOPHIA. It does seem very far away... and a long time ago.

DANILO. Nearly five years now.
[*Pause. Sophia smiles.*]

9

SOPHIA. That's right. Five years. Said like that it doesn't sound long, does it?

DANILO. Do you miss it?

SOPHIA. The city? No. Life is much slower and simpler here, but once you get used to it, the days are as full as they were anywhere.

DANILO. And Dimetos?

SOPHIA. Miss the city? I don't think so. It would be simple enough to return if he did.

DANILO. He's kept busy then, is he?

SOPHIA. I wouldn't say that either. It's not every day that we have a horse at the bottom of a well.

DANILO. Don't the people around here know who he is?

SOPHIA. Yes.

DANILO. They're fools not to use him.

SOPHIA. City reputations don't count for much in these parts. But when the need arises they come to him for help as you can see.

DANILO. Dimetos not busy! Another surprise.

SOPHIA. You knew him well.

DANILO. No. We met once a long time ago. He won't even remember. But I'd heard about him like everyone else, and from what I'd heard I wouldn't have believed he could be happy if he wasn't working.

SOPHIA. I didn't say he was happy... [*She smiles easily at Danilo.*] I'm not saying he's unhappy. Our life here is also without extremes. The climate has enough of those.

DANILO. Is it always as dry as this?

SOPHIA. This summer has been particularly bad. They've already started praying for rain.

DANILO. They might do better asking Dimetos to build them a dam.

SOPHIA. Don't let them hear you say that. They take their religion very seriously. If there is one respect in which they haven't accepted the three of us, it is our seeming negligence in that direction.

DANILO. Dimetos, Lydia... and you of course are Sophia.

SOPHIA. His housekeeper.

DANILO. You've been with him a long time, haven't you?

SOPHIA. I started working for his mother when I was seventeen. He

10

was ten. But I'm sure you knew that as well.

DANILO. Yes, I did. I tried to find out as much as I could before I came here.

SOPHIA [stops working]. What do you want?

DANILO. That's obvious surely.

SOPHIA. Dimetos.

DANILO. We need him. It's as simple and selfish as that. We've woken up to realize what should have been obvious years ago: that unless a few things are done very quickly our 'bustling little metropolis' is going to be in very serious trouble. My particular responsibility is one he knows all about—water, thirsty people . . .

SOPHIA. Is there a shortage of engineers?

DANILO. His sort, yes. There are plenty of others who know as much, a few who are even as experienced. Dimetos is remembered and talked about by men because he had something else as well . . . a quality we're running dangerously short of. Vision. That's why I'm here. What chance do I have persuading him to return? He can dictate his own terms.

SOPHIA [*reflectively*]. I don't know. [*Danilo is watching her.*] I don't. All I can suggest is that you try, and find out.

DANILO. You are pessimistic about my chances.

SOPHIA. I don't know enough to be pessimistic or optimistic. He's a very private man. He never talks about going back.

DANILO. But he can't mean to spend the rest of his life here.

SOPHIA. Why not?

DANILO. It doesn't make sense. No more than his departure did.

SOPHIA [*speaking easily enough, but with a sensed undercurrent*]. What is so strange in a man retiring to the peace and quiet?

DANILO. Retire? It wasn't an old man that suddenly packed up and left us. I don't doubt that it's peaceful and quiet here but for a man like him that's as pointless as a grave.

SOPHIA. Choose your words carefully in talking to him.

DANILO. Forgive me. My bad manners and impatience are a measure of how much we need him.

SOPHIA. There are men here as well. He's helping one at this moment.

DANILO. I admitted to being selfish. Cities have no morality except their own survival. [*He tries again.*] I know it will be pointless asking him to come back if he doesn't want to. But I'm hoping

he does. That our selfish need will coincide with what he wants
SOPHIA. You'll know the answer to that soon enough. They shouldn'
be long now. Will you excuse me? [*Exit.*]
DANILO [*alone*]. Prayers for rain. 'On your knees sinners. You'v
done it again.' Nothing as good as a little human misery to high
light the mysterious workings of His will being done on Our earth
Dimetos! What are you doing here! [*He thinks.*] They showed m
a stone wall ... three miles long, shoulder height. The stones wer
hewn from the local rock. Every one shaped ... chisel and hamme
of course ... to interlock perfectly with the next. There's not
trowel of mortar in its entire length. It really is beautiful. *A*
mosaic with cellular depth, as if living tissue had been its inspira
tion. And strong. It no longer serves any purpose yet it defie
dereliction. You could walk the length of it comfortably in ... a
hour? It was built a long time ago by two slaves and it took then
their entire lifetimes. 'Men don't build like that anymore!' I wa
told proudly. [*Pause.*] No they don't. It costs too much. That wal
isn't made of stone. Fear. That's why it's still there. A monumen
to man's capacity to stand still.

Scene 4

Dimetos, *hanging ropes and pulleys from a roof beam above the table*
and Danilo.

DIMETOS. What do you mean? 'Hard to find'? The only red tiled roo
in the village, two cypresses in front and an old mulberry tre
next to the house. What could be simpler?
DANILO. Looking for a prophet in the wilderness. To start with thi
village isn't even marked on the map I was using. And when I di
find it—well, the locals even seem to resent their neighbou
having a name. A lesser man than you could easily be lost to th
world out here. What made you choose it?
DIMETOS. I had a workman once, from this valley. A strange man
He handled a tool as if he had personally declared war on matter
So I put him charge of the quarries. He assaulted that rock as i
nothing short of its total obliteration would satisfy him. It was
clever move. He produced stone faster than we could use it. H

was very typical of this region. Without that dour tenacity of purpose, survival here wouldn't be possible.

ANILO. I suppose that's the most that can be hoped for out here.

IMETOS. Don't be too hard on them. They get a little living done as well. It's a harsh environment, but not impossible.

ANILO. It depresses me. It seems to invite the brutal response you described in your workman.
Who do you talk to, Dimetos?

IMETOS. Talk! I didn't come here for that.

ANILO. Obviously. I can't help wondering what did bring you here.

IMETOS. They might be simple around here, Danilo—how else will you describe them when you get back? Primitive? Uncultured?— but their needs are real. If anything more so just because life is basic. When a man needs water here he doesn't look for a tap, he digs a well. And having dug that well he must get the water to the top, and having got it there he must get it to his lands. It might all seem very obvious to you, but that is exactly what fascinates me. Problems your citizens have forgotten about, solutions to those problems which I had taken for granted, are again very real issues. It's refreshing, Danilo. Stimulating.

That's not to mention the further challenge of getting a new idea past the barriers of habit and prejudice. Their tools, techniques, are crude and inefficient. But they're the ones their fathers put into their hands and taught them how to use. To suggest modifying them not only demands a new dexterity of the wrist, but also of the soul. It's almost sacrilege. I haven't been all that successful, but they're learning to trust me. They've started to knock on my door when the need arises.

ANILO. That's what I'm doing.

IMETOS. You've come a long way to do that.

ANILO. It's a big need. Didn't Sophia tell you why I'm here?

IMETOS. No.

ANILO. But you can guess.

IMETOS. Yes. Don't waste your time, Danilo.

ANILO. I owe it to more than just myself to try.

IMETOS. I don't want to waste mine either.

ANILO. But you haven't even heard what I've got to say?

IMETOS. Because there's nothing you could that would make me want to return.

DANILO. The city doesn't mean anything to you any more?

DIMETOS. Nothing.

[*Pause.*]

DANILO[*not knowing what to say*]. Well ...

DIMETOS. I've shocked you.

DANILO. Yes, you have. I came prepared to argue about a lot of things, but not that.

DIMETOS. What should it 'mean' to me, Danilo. Do I owe something?

DANILO. That wasn't what I was going to say.

DIMETOS. All right ... what were you going to?

DANILO. I don't think there is any point to it now.

DIMETOS. Your city is simply more people in one place than anywhere else. And if it's to people I owe something—which I don't think I do—there are enough of them here for me to repay my debt in full. You must understand, Danilo. If I'd wanted to engineer another project for your citizens I'd be back among them. I wasn't forced to leave and I'm not being kept here against my will. Both were choices. Eat with us before you go. The news you take back mustn't be that I have also abandoned my manners.

[*Exit Danilo. After a few seconds alone, Dimetos is joined by Sophia. He looks up expectantly as she enters.*]

Where's Lydia?

SOPHIA. Washing mud out of her hair, and singing. I don't think I've seen her so happy.

DIMETOS. She's got every reason to be. If it wasn't for her, that horse would still be down there. None of the men was prepared to do it.

SOPHIA. Did she really take off her clothes in front of them?

DIMETOS. It would have been impossible otherwise. She wouldn't have been able to move.

SOPHIA. That will give them something to talk about in the village. I go cold every time I think of her at the end of that rope.

DIMETOS. I knew what I was doing.

SOPHIA. I don't doubt that.

DIMETOS. I've asked Danilo to eat with us.

SOPHIA. I thought you might. I've prepared enough. [*Watching him.*] He's upset you, hasn't he?

DIMETOS. Is it that obvious?

SOPHIA. I would have been surprised if he hadn't. He told me what he had come to see you about. Asked me what I thought of his chances.

DIMETOS. And?

SOPHIA. And what?

DIMETOS. What did you say to him?

SOPHIA. The truth. That I didn't know.

DIMETOS. Why do you smile?

SOPHIA. I think it's the first time I couldn't guess what your response would be . . . not that I would have told him if I had.

DIMETOS. The answer was 'No'.

SOPHIA. So I gathered. Then why does he still bother you? Didn't he accept it?

DIMETOS. He had no choice. I have no intention of going back. Even when I've disagreed, or haven't understood, I've always respected other men's decisions as to how they wanted to live their lives. Is that asking too much for myself?

SOPHIA. Wasn't he respectful? I thought there was more than enough of that for Dimetos the Engineer. He came a long way to see you.

DIMETOS. He should have spared himself the trouble.

SOPHIA [*quietly*]. I'm not persuading you to return.
[*Pause.*]

DIMETOS. I'm sorry, Sophia. I'm not even angry with him. It's myself. I lied to him.

SOPHIA. I know. [*He looks at her.*] I couldn't help hearing. I wouldn't worry too much about it though. I don't think he realized.

DIMETOS. Of course he didn't. It was a very convincing performance. I almost believed it myself. 'Dimetos is working! And his inspiration? Another man's need.'

SOPHIA. That was certainly true once.

DIMETOS. I'm not even sure of that any more. [*She is watching him.*] Desertion does more than just terminate a loyalty, Sophia. It makes a lie of whatever loyalty there had been.

SOPHIA. Those are strong words.

DIMETOS. I am sure that is how Danilo sees it.

SOPHIA. Is he right? [*Dimetos makes a vague gesture.*] That's how you see it.

DIMETOS. Sometimes. I know you are very patient, Sophia, but have you ever felt provoked to asking me 'What are you doing here?'

SOPHIA. Have you been waiting for me to?

DIMETOS. I would have thought it an obvious question by now.

SOPHIA. I did ask it . . . a long time ago and not here, but it was the same question. The day you came home and told me you were leaving. I was surprised. I'd been expecting something but nothing quite as abrupt and final as that. I asked you, why? Only once . . . I didn't need to a second time because you never stopped answering me. You were tired, you needed a change, the stimulus of fresh challenges . . . Are you saying none of that was true?

DIMETOS. It wasn't as simple or as blatant as that. I *was* tired at the time. No, I'm saying that I used that to hide, from myself, something else.

[*Pause. She waits.*]

SOPHIA. Do I have to ask?

DIMETOS. No. It's not easy to know where or how to start. This afternoon at the well. Lydia had secured the ropes and was safely up. Everyone stood around waiting. I checked everything for the last time—the tripod, pulleys—all were fine. There was nothing left to do except try. So we tensed the rope, just enough to feel the weight of the animal at the other end. We dug in our heels . . . Lydia joined us . . . made sure of our hold on the rope. Then I gave the word and we pulled. It was remarkable. At that precise moment, when we all strained in unison, it was as if our faces and names disappeared. All that mattered was what each of us, trying his utmost, could contribute. And our individual efforts brought to a simple focus by that rope. It worked. Hand over hand we brought him up, a few inches at a time. It's been long since I experienced the excitement I felt at that moment. It used to be like that all the time. Do you realize there must have been an actual moment in history, one specific place and time when something on two legs picked up a stone and used it for the first time— smashed a bone so that he could get at the marrow? We've come a long way since then, but that moment this afternoon was part of the campaign that started with that first blow. [*He indicates his table and tools.*] The armoury—six mechanical powers—lever, pulley, inclined plane, wedge, screw and wheel. That's what they are. The tools and machines I've used or put into other men's hands ... extensions to those hands, giving them new powers in their defiance of a universe that resists us. The battle cry: Help men Defy!

There is nothing more beautiful than a man making something and making it well, than a pair of hands urgent and quick with a need and behind those a guiding intelligence. Do you know what bridges that mysterious distance between head and hands, bringing them so close together that they are almost one? Caring. Not the most exciting of words is it? Almost as humble as a tool. But that is the Alchemist's Stone of human endeavour. I know what I'm talking about, Sophia, because mine were like that, head and hands fused, alloyed to a point where you couldn't separate the action of the one from the intention of the other. And they were like that because I 'cared'. Not about the city, but about people. [*He pauses. Sophia is listening carefully.*]

SOPHIA [*before he can continue*]. Don't say anything you are going to regret.

DIMETOS. It would only be a question of hearing the words aloud. I've already said it to myself. I don't care any more. Don't ask me why because I don't know. But something eroded away the habit of caring. I carried on behaving as if I still did, until the lie became intolerable. [*He picks up a tool from the table.*] Usage blunts a tool, but when that happens you sharpen it, when it wears out you replace it. It's not as simple as that with ...

SOPHIA. The heart, Dimetos.

DIMETOS. Head, hands, and heart. It's easier here only because I don't have to lie to myself, or others. I do what little work comes my way, dispense what little help I can because it's a civilized habit, not a passion. And even then ... ! If I'd been my self this morning I might well have left that horse and those squabbling idiots to their predicament.

SOPHIA. Lydia.

DIMETOS. Yes. She was very upset when she saw the animal.

SOPHIA. Your caring hasn't stopped completely then.

DIMETOS. I don't 'care' about Lydia... [*Sophia waits.*] I love her as if she were my own child.
[*Exit Dimetos. Sophia is alone and thoughtful for a few seconds before Lydia enters.*]

LYDIA. Sophia, it's dry now. [*She sits and hands Sophia her hairbrush.*] Who is the visitor?

SOPHIA. A young man from the city. [*Tapping Lydia on the head with the brush.*] Come on. [*She brushes Lydia's hair while they play their 'game'.*]

LYDIA [*closing her eyes and thinking*]. Yes! The sunlight when I came out of the well.

SOPHIA. One.

LYDIA. The horse galloping away from me.

SOPHIA. Two.

LYDIA. I saw a pig.

SOPHIA. What's beautiful about a pig?

LYDIA. He had two big pink ears.

[*They laugh.*]

SOPHIA. Three.

LYDIA. I found a beautiful stone by the pool.

SOPHIA. Four.

LYDIA. I heard someone whistling.

SOPHIA. Five.

LYDIA. I saw a small cloud far away.

SOPHIA. Six.

LYDIA. I looked at that big tree in the meadow again. It is still beautiful.

SOPHIA. Seven.

LYDIA. The sunset on our way home.

SOPHIA. Eight.

LYDIA. Our house as we came over the hill.

SOPHIA. Nine.

LYDIA [*pausing to think, then quietly*]. Your hands when you brush my hair.

SOPHIA. Ten. [*She embraces Lydia.*]

Scene 5

The garden. Lydia *and* Danilo.

LYDIA. It was more than thirty foot deep. We measured it afterwards. When we got there they were all just standing around arguing about whose fault it was. The old man who owned the horse said that the man who owned the well was to blame because the fence around it was rotten, but the man who owned the well said the man who owned the horse...

DANILO. ...said that the man who owned the well said that the man who owned the horse said that the man who owned the well...

LYDIA [*laughing*]. That's right! Nobody was trying to do anything. There's a saying here that whoever throws the first stone must take responsibility for the last...only it wasn't stones they were offering each other but big rocks. They were going to kill him. We just listened at first. Then my uncle got very angry. I've never seen him like that before. 'Use your hands you bloody idiots, not your tongues.' He just pushed them aside and went to work. While he was putting up the ropes and pulleys he made them dig a slope down into it—he called it a ramp—so that the horse could climb out when we got him half way up. I could see none of them thought it was going to work but they were too frightened of him to argue.

DANILO. And you?

LYDIA. Frightened of my uncle?

DANILO. No. Did you think it was going to work?

LYDIA. Of course. He doesn't do anything unless it will work. And it did. The first time, with all of them pulling.

DANILO. You're a loyal apprentice. One way or another it has certainly been a day of surprises. None of the young women I know spend their time pulling horses out of wells.

LYDIA. It's the first time I've really helped him. I usually just get in the way.

DANILO. I'm sure that's not true.

LYDIA. Yes, it is. He's very patient though. Always pretends I've been a big help.

DANILO. What else do you do?

LYDIA. Help Sophia in the house. I think I get in the way there too sometimes.

DANILO. Dimetos and Sophia. Anybody else?

LYDIA. Not really.

DANILO. It must be lonely for you.

LYDIA. I'm used to it now. Just when I really start getting bored something happens . . . last year there were floods, today it was the horse. That makes up for everything.

DANILO. You might have to wait a long time before that happens again.

LYDIA. No! I'd rather have nothing to do. What did you come to see my uncle about?

DANILO. I was hoping to persuade him to return to the city. Help us to rescue some of our horses. [*Lydia smiles.*] I wish it was a joke. But the truth is we also just stand around looking at our disasters, arguing whose fault it was and doing nothing. The only difference is that it is not horses who are in trouble but people.

LYDIA. He'll help you if he can.

DANILO. Oh he certainly can, but he won't.

LYDIA. Why do you say that?

DANILO. Because he told me. Life here is far too exciting and challenging for him to think of leaving.

LYDIA. My uncle said that?

DANILO. Words to that effect. Didn't you know it? You look as surprised as I was.

LYDIA [*confused*]. He . . . we never talk about it. I've always just taken it for granted that . . .

DANILO. This was home?

LYDIA. Yes.

DANILO. You'd like to go back, wouldn't you?

LYDIA. Yes.

DANILO. At last! Somebody on my side. Sophia was also indifferent to the prospect.

LYDIA. She'll go wherever Dimetos goes.

DANILO. So I gathered.

LYDIA [*with a defiant note in her voice*]. So will I!

DANILO. I'm not arguing with you. I'm disappointed that's all. We really could use your uncle.

LYDIA. Did you try very hard?

DANILO. No. I got off to a bad start by antagonizing Sophia. And when it came to Dimetos ... well he wouldn't even let me speak. It was almost as if ... [*Pause.*]

LYDIA. What?

DANILO. You'll get angry with me if I say it.

LYDIA. I can't be your friend if you don't like him.

DANILO. I respect him, Lydia. I wouldn't have come all this way if I didn't.

LYDIA. I know I should be happy here. We've got everything we need.

DANILO. Maybe you haven't. There's no disloyalty in that. I'm sure they'd be the first to admit it. You're younger than them, that's all. And the city's got more to offer someone with a life still to be lived.

LYDIA. I think I've forgotten what it looks like.

DANILO. You'll find it changed. Five years is a long time in a city's life.

LYDIA. Bigger?

DANILO. Much.

LYDIA. More people?

DANILO. Too many!

LYDIA. And happy people!
[*They laugh.*]

DANILO. Your villagers certainly are a serious lot.

LYDIA. I didn't mind it when we first came here. Everything was different and strange. I'm sure my uncle felt that way too. We had all sorts of plans and schemes. We built the footbridge across the river in that first year. None of them would use it at first. I used to run up and down it to prove it was safe. But some of the old people are still waiting for it to fall. [*Pause.*]

DANILO. What's the matter?

LYDIA. Just thinking ... it was good to have something to do again today. [*Turning to Danilo.*] I think you gave up too easily. Every-body does that with him.

DANILO. He's a very formidable man.

LYDIA. Not really. Why don't you try again?

DANILO. I wouldn't know where to start.

LYDIA. I'll help you. I'll tell him I want to go back. Sometimes he does things for me when he's already said no to others.

DANILO. I can understand why. All right.

Scene 6

The meal. Dimetos, Danilo, Sophia *and* Lydia *are sitting round the table.*

DIMETOS [*to Danilo*]. They've left the old fort intact?

DANILO. Intact? It's become impregnable. A wave of historical necro–philia swept through us a few years ago. We dug up the bones of every hero we could find and reburied them inside its walls. Reverence as well as history now protects it.

DIMETOS. I remember sitting up there one day, looking down. You could see a lot of the city from up there—the road through the valley, all the way down to the harbour. From that height the people were no bigger than ants, the traffic a child's game with little toys. I wondered what the correct analogy was for what I was looking at. Organic or mechanical? The complexity of it! That system of roads, like arteries, with life flowing along them. Was the city finally an organism, something more than just the sum total of all the individual lives it contained ... or was it still only a machine, a system of forces that could be controlled?

DANILO. What did you decide?

DIMETOS. I didn't. Because a third possibility occurred to me. That I was looking at the creation of a modern Daedalus into which Theseus has gone without his ball of twine.

DANILO. That image could be read as either pessimistic or a challenge to us to get out of our mess but this time without any help from the gods.

DIMETOS. That depends on how clever our unaided Theseus is, doesn't it?

DANILO. I think he stands a chance. After all the labyrinth, for all its intricacies, remains man-made. In fact that little part of it you looked down on, has now been unmade. Most of it has been demolished and cleared for re–development.

IMETOS. I suppose that was inevitable.

ANILO. It was long overdue. I don't share your affection for it. I've also stood up there and looked down, but all I saw was a slum. People crowded together in conditions that made a decent life impossible, and our efforts to give them that frustrated by prejudice and sentiment. I'm cast in the role of the Villain these days, Dimetos. Progress has become a dirty word.

OPHIA. I'm one of those who are suspicious of it.

ANILO. Why?

OPHIA. The schemes get bigger and and bigger, the people smaller. It's become so soulless, Danilo, like the masses of concrete it always entails.

ANILO. Concrete is a mixture of sand and cement. It's the architects who are supposed to have the souls, and I'll be the first to admit that a lot of them design as if they didn't. Why reduce what we are trying to do, what we have *got* to do, to that one, very useful material.

OPHIA. There is so much of it.

ANILO. Because there are a lot of people Sophia! We haven't got the luxury of time any more. Maybe we never had it. There might be a definition there. Man is the only animal to be trapped by time. That's the real labyrinth and to get out of it we have got to plan and build very fast, and bigger than before. [*Turning to Lydia.*] Are you frightened of progress?

OPHIA. I said I was 'suspicious'.

YDIA [*uncertainly*]. I don't know.

ANILO. It's only a word. It means to move forward . . . to try and live your life in the only direction it has got—tomorrow! How do you feel about tomorrow?

YDIA. Good.

ANILO. Why?

YDIA. I don't know . . . No, I do! Because today was good.

ANILO. And if it had been bad?

YDIA. I'd try very hard to make tomorrow better.

ANILO. So one way or another, you want tomorrow.

YDIA. Oh, yes!

ANILO. You believe in progress.

YDIA. Do I?

23

DANILO. Oh, yes.

LYDIA. But I also agree with Sophia. I don't like concrete. I pref
bricks.

DANILO. Then build with bricks. We use them as well. Get Dimet
to build you a house of real bricks down in the valley. Wou
you like that?

LYDIA. Yes.

[*She looks at Dimetos. He has been watching the exchange betwe*
her and Danilo, quietly. Sophia has been watching him. He spea
easily enough in reply to Lydia's look.]

DIMETOS. Not in the valley. I spent too much of my youth in thos
streets. There are ghosts waiting for me there.

LYDIA. Good or bad?

DIMETOS. They were good men.

LYDIA. Then they'll be good ghosts! Who are they?

DIMETOS. The people who lived there.

LYDIA. You've never mentioned them before.

DIMETOS. Haven't I? I used to walk around down there ... watc
them live and work. [*Lydia is waiting expectantly.*] A man calle
Jerome ... a potter. Yes! His hands would certainly be a ghost
those streets if I ever went back there. [*Remembering.*] Slende
but surprisingly firm and strong. The clay hadn't softened ther
I can still see him wiping them on his apron before greeting me .
and then giving them back to work. I used to watch them whi
we talked. And we did, without interrupting them at all. In tho
hands the clay became something that combined the virtues
both liquid and solid. It flowed or stayed just as he wanted.

Or Daniel! There was a different pair of hands. The differen
between clay and metal, between finger tips and the impact of
four-pound hammer wielded by an arm as thick as a man's thig
But they also knew their business. The last time I saw him I
was at work on a chain—for one of the ships in the harbour
forging each link as if it was the one destined for Prometheus.

The pair I think I'll remember longest though did not belor
to a worker. They were also very accomplished in their busines
as sure in their grasp as Daniel's and as effortless in their actic
as Jerome's. But they produced nothing, unless you can count t
gasp of a throng of spectators as produce. A juggler! A circ

pitched its tent in one of those vacant lots one year. A sad little show—a few flea-bitten goats who could spell their names—but they also had a juggler. In explaining his trade to me he posed a paradox: 'Learn to give and take with the same action.'

ANILO. What about a beggar's hands?

METOS. Beggars take, what do they give? I have no patience with that bloodless ethic that elevates beggary to a state of Grace.

ANILO. Almost your exact words! About ten years ago. My first and only meeting with you before today. You don't remember.

METOS. No.

ANILO. The market square. The storm-water system. You were very busy, irritable... you hadn't been given enough workmen, the equipment was inadequate... [*He smiles at the memory of himself.*] A very junior official added to your irritation by asking for an inventory of the materials you had on site. You told me exactly what you thought about inventories, turned your back on me and stumbled over a beggar. Your anger was magnificent! 'What do you give men back for their charity! Blessings won't hold bricks together. Your hands can still work. You blaspheme them by begging.'

METOS. You've got a good memory, Danilo.

ANILO. It's a moment I don't want to forget, as you haven't forgotten yours. Those few words made me realize what it meant to be a man among other men. A reciprocity, not of tears, but sweat.

METOS. A stirring vision.

ANILO. It is, isn't it? At times we come close to making it our reality.

METOS. They were rare occasions when I was there. Most of what passed as 'vision' could be better summed up in the word profit.

NILO. That is still very much the case, but there are exceptions... as you were.

METOS. You flatter me, Danilo. All I ever did...

NILO [*cutting him short*]. No! We're playing games with each other Dimetos. I respect you too much to 'waste your time' yet again and in that fashion. I am going to risk your anger. I don't believe what you said to me about being here. I don't know whether you are lying to me or yourself, but I cannot believe that pulling old plough horses out of wells or being an odd-job man to a crowd of peasants satisfies you. Do you know what you're keeping

company with here? An abject and servile dependence on super
stition and religion that reduces man and denies history. That
what I'm really asking you to come back to...

LYDIA [*moving impulsively towards Dimetos*]. Please listen to him.

DIMETOS. I have. Very carefully.

LYDIA. That's what I mean...don't be angry. Yes, you are! Bu
don't be. Maybe it is time for us to return.

DIMETOS [*smiling at her then moving away*]. I think I do rememb
that beggar. If those were my words they certainly didn't hav
any effect on him. He was still sitting around in the sun when w
finished there. I wouldn't be surprised if he was still. Yes, tho
empty hands always angered me. They seemed to betray th
'vision' more significantly than your profiteers ever will. It's n
pleasant to see a man end up that useless. [*Turning to Danilo
Don't go tomorrow. Give me time to think.

DANILO. As much time as you need.

SOPHIA. It's late, Lydia.

LYDIA. Not yet. [*She looks at Dimetos.*] Just a little longer.

SOPHIA [*to Danilo*]. I'll show you to your room.

DANILO [*to Dimetos*]. Goodnight. [*To Lydia.*]...and thank you.
[*Exeunt Sophia and Danilo.*]

LYDIA. This is the happiest day of my life. I don't want it to en
First the horse, then a visitor, and now...

DIMETOS. All I said...

LYDIA. I know! But please think hard...Dimetos.

DIMETOS. The two of you left me no choice.

LYDIA. Are you cross with me?

DIMETOS. For what reason?

LYDIA. Being on his side. He told me what he'd come to see yo
about. I made him try again.

DIMETOS. I see. So that is what inspired our young visionary. Yo
like him?

LYDIA. Yes. [*She pulls down an end of rope hanging from the roof bea
and ties a knot.*] And you?

DIMETOS. Yes.

LYDIA. He does respect you. I'd like him for that alone.

DIMETOS. But he's also handsome, he made you laugh and now th thought of him is making you blush. Don't be embarrassed. I've thought of you as the little one for too long. You're a young woman and Danilo is a young man. It's as simple as that.

LYDIA [*finishing the knot*]. Now pull it tight...and it doesn't slip. That's right, isn't it—the knot we used this morning?

DIMETOS. Yes. Perfect.

LYDIA. I didn't even have to think. My hands will never forget how to tie it.

DIMETOS. The Fisherman's Bend. It can't slip because the knot will tighten and bite into itself when subjected to strain.

LYDIA. Teach me another. [*He sits beside her.*] Slowly...

DIMETOS [*ties a knot*]. There. Figure of eight.

LYDIA. Let me try.

DIMETOS [*watching*]. That's not what a young woman should be applying her hands to. Let me see them. [*Looks at her hands.*] The ones that worked for me were calloused and rough with biographies of hard work and tools. Men's hands. These...have a different purpose waiting for them.

What would you like to do with them?

LYDIA. Use them the way I did today.

DIMETOS. No. We don't want any callouses on these. They're meant for other skills than pulling old plough horses out of wells.

LYDIA. He's not a plough horse. You know that.

DIMETOS. That's what Danilo called him. And what was I? Handyman to a crowd of peasants! He wasn't exactly the model of tact in his persuasion was he?

[*Lydia watches Dimetos in silence for a few seconds.*]

LYDIA. You don't like him.

DIMETOS. I don't dislike him. He's given me a lot to think about, that's all.

LYDIA. And you are still cross with me.

DIMETOS. Don't be silly.

[*Lydia goes up to him and faces him with simple and total honesty.*]

LYDIA. I owe you everything. If I thought you were happy here, I wouldn't have interfered.

DIMETOS. What makes you think I'll be happy back in the city?

LYDIA. Work. He was right. People need you.

DIMETOS. I'm tired of other men's needs, other men's disasters.

LYDIA. I don't believe that. You wouldn't have saved the horse th
morning if that was true.

DIMETOS. I saved that horse for you! [*Looks at her.*] You understan
and see so much, and yet you're so blind to other things. [*Pause*
Yes, I saved that horse for you. I knotted those ropes around you
waist and lowered you because I had sworn to myself I was goin
to pull your pain out of the world. But what started off with suc
grim determination then became the most remarkable thing I'v
ever seen. He succumbed to you! Stood absolutely still while yo
straddled him and went to work. There was one moment whe
you were prostrate on his back, your cheek resting on his powerf
neck, your hands working away quietly underneath him as yo
placed the slings ... both of you covered in mud! Yes, that was i
Two bodies separate and yet mysteriously at one with each other
I wonder what memory the animal has of that moment ... at t
bottom of a dark hole, too stupid to believe in the possibility
help ... frightened ... and then something so light and beautif
coming to your rescue. If I was an artist I'd turn my hand
modelling that. Try to capture the contrast between the powerf
contours of his helplessness and the delicacy of your determinatio
[*Pause. Exit abruptly.*]

Scene 7

The garden. Dimetos *and* Sophia.

SOPHIA. More wine?

DIMETOS. No. I've had too much already.

SOPHIA. Have you got work to do?

DIMETOS. Yes. But my head is not very clear.

SOPHIA. I hope it was when you asked him to stay on. You chang
your mind very quickly.

DIMETOS. I didn't change my mind, Sophia! All I said ...

SOPHIA. I know ... you are going to think about it. [*Something in
tone makes Dimetos look at her.*] Please work. I enjoy watchi
your hands.

DIMETOS. I don't know that I can trust them tonight.
[*Pause.*]

SOPHIA. The dogs are very noisy.

DIMETOS. I haven't noticed.

SOPHIA. Listen. They make the night sound full of trouble, don't they? When we first came here I use to lie and listen and wonder what mischief there could be in a place like this to keep them so busy.

DIMETOS. Shadows.

SOPHIA. But of what? Shadows aren't things in themselves. There's always something else isn't there, something more real ... even if it's only a thought. It's all we know about them sometimes; and then, like dogs, raise our hackles and bark.

DIMETOS. You're in a strange mood, Sophia.

SOPHIA. I suppose I am. Must be the heat. These summers have never got any easier. I'll be glad when the cooler weather comes.

DIMETOS. A few more days to the solstice.

SOPHIA. You haven't been sleeping too well either have you? I've heard you moving around the house at night.

DIMETOS. Like you I find this weather very uncomfortable.
[*Pause. He looks up to find Sophia staring at him.*]

SOPHIA. You don't trust me do you?

DIMETOS. What makes you say that?

SOPHIA. Because you don't.

DIMETOS. I don't know what you're talking about, Sophia.

SOPHIA. Maybe I've also had too much wine. Lydia will sleep soundly though won't she ... after her busy day. The sleep of the innocent.

DIMETOS. What are we guilty of?

SOPHIA. Our lives, if nothing else.

DIMETOS. All we've done is live them.

SOPHIA. Speak for yourself. A dedicated servant ends up without a life of her own.

DIMETOS. Where does that word come from suddenly?

SOPHIA. Which one?

DIMETOS. You know the one I mean. I've never called you or thought of you as that.

SOPHIA. But it's true, isn't it? If I'm not a servant what am I? Mother?

29

Sister? I'm not old enough for the first and I've never thoug
of myself as the second. There's also 'friend' 'companion' . . . if th
others are too personal. How do *you* see me Dimetos? Who am I

DIMETOS. Sophia.

SOPHIA. Faithful, loyal, trustworthy Sophia!

DIMETOS. You have been all of those.

SOPHIA. They are the virtues of a good servant.

Scene 8

Lydia *wakes with a scream.*

LYDIA. DIMETOS! [*Pause. Then softly.*] Sophia! Sophia!
[*Sophia enters and starts brushing her hair. The mood between t
two of them is muted and in strong contrast to their first scene togethe*
Your turn.

SOPHIA [*hollowly*]. The first light in our room this morning.

LYDIA. One.

SOPHIA. The fire in the stove.

LYDIA. Two.

SOPHIA. Water . . .
[*Lydia shakes her head. Sophia abandons the game.*]

LYDIA. What's happening?

SOPHIA. I don't understand.

LYDIA. Something is happening to us.

SOPHIA. We're waiting for Dimetos to make up his mind. While
is doing that you are entertaining Danilo and doing it very well

LYDIA. Is that all?

SOPHIA. Isn't that enough for you?
[*Pause.*]

LYDIA. Your hands seem different, Sophia.

SOPHIA. In what way?

LYDIA. It's hard to imagine you when I feel them.

SOPHIA. I'm doing it as I've always done it.

LYDIA. You're not hurting . . . but it's as if I don't know them, a
they don't know me.

Let me look at you?

SOPHIA [*avoiding her eyes*]. You're very strange, Lydia. Let me finish. I have work waiting.

LYDIA. Look at me. Smile.

SOPHIA. I don't feel like smiling today.

[*Pause.*]

LYDIA. Uncle is also avoiding me.

SOPHIA. What do you mean?

LYDIA. He just ...

SOPHIA. What do you mean?

LYDIA. I don't know.

[*Pause.*]

SOPHIA. You're still hoping he will decide to go back.

LYDIA. Of course. Why do you say it like that? Aren't you?

SOPHIA. It's not important to me ... and if it was I would quickly stop it being so. Because he won't.

LYDIA. Did he tell you that?

SOPHIA. No.

LYDIA. Then what makes you so sure?

SOPHIA. I've been with him longer than you. Sometimes I know his mind even before he does.

LYDIA. Is this one of those times?

SOPHIA. Yes.

[*Pause.*]

LYDIA. You're saying he's lying.

SOPHIA. Yes. Didn't you think he could?

LYDIA. Why is he?

SOPHIA. That's his business.

LYDIA. Don't you know that as well?

SOPHIA. I don't want to know.

[*Pause.*]

LYDIA. It's still your turn.

SOPHIA [*mechanically*]. Butterfly ... bird ... rainbow ...

LYDIA [*shaking her head*]. No ...

SOPHIA. I saw a dead dog.

LYDIA. That's enough Sophia. Thank you.

SOPHIA [*stops brushing Lydia's hair*]. Be careful little one. [*Exit.*]

31

Scene 9

Beside the pool. Lydia *and* Danilo.

DANILO [*off-stage*]. Lydia! Lydia! [*He enters. He has obviously had
too much to drink.*] Why did you run away?

LYDIA. I didn't run, I walked.

DANILO. You know what I mean. One moment you were there
and when I looked again...

LYDIA. I wasn't enjoying myself.

DANILO. It wasn't that bad. In fact, I was pleasantly surprised to
see what a few glasses of wine could do for these 'stern sons of
the soil'. One of them even had a joke. You believe that? 'What's
the difference between a duck?' Well?

LYDIA. I don't know.

DANILO. One of its legs is both the same! [*He laughs at himself.*]
Danilo... you're a long way from home.

LYDIA. Have a swim. You'll feel better.

DANILO [*laughing*]. Better? That is absolutely impossible. I feel better
than I have ever felt. You look clean and fresh and I...

LYDIA. You have had too much wine.

DANILO. That... is putting it mildly. [*Pause.*] How long have I been
here now?

LYDIA. Five days.

DANILO. You sure?

LYDIA. Yes. Does it seem longer or shorter?

DANILO. I don't know. I honestly don't know. That's a bad sign
isn't it? No sense of time! That's how it starts.

LYDIA. What?

DANILO [*stops himself in time*]. Nothing. This little valley of yours
a dangerous place. I felt it the day I arrived. A man's sense of
purpose could end up as stunted as the thorn trees out there
he stayed here too long.

LYDIA. Like my uncle.

DANILO [*making a vague gesture*]. We'll water his purposes back
life. [*Lydia moves.*] What's the matter?

LYDIA. I thought I saw someone.

DANILO. Where?

32

LYDIA. Among those lemon trees.

DANILO. So?

LYDIA. So I thought I saw someone.

DANILO [*finally registering her depressed mood*]. What's wrong?

LYDIA. Nothing.

DANILO. I'm not that drunk, little one. Or are you saying it's none of my business?

LYDIA. No. It is. You must go, Danilo. You are wasting your time. Dimetos won't go back.

DANILO. You certainly are down. Don't be such a pessimist. I had a word with him back there. He's promised to give me his decision tonight.

LYDIA. That is what he will tell you.

DANILO. What?

LYDIA. Please listen, Danilo. He is not going back to the city.

DANILO. Don't make me think, Lydia. This sun is very hot. [*Pause.*] When did he tell you?

LYDIA. He didn't. It was Sophia.

DANILO. He told her?

LYDIA. No.

DANILO. That's her guess.

LYDIA. It's not just a guess. She . . .

DANILO. What makes you think she's right?

LYDIA. Please Danilo! Dimetos is not going back.

DANILO. All right! Well . . . that's rather abrupt and sobering. I thought I had succeeded. Mission accomplished! He put up a damned good performance of having not yet decided. 'We'll thrash out the whole matter tonight.' Come to think of it he did get away from me in a hurry. Well? Aren't you going to make me try again?

LYDIA. No.

DANILO. Sorry, Lydia. The sarcasm was really directed at myself.

LYDIA. I should never have interfered.

DANILO. Interfered?

LYDIA. If I hadn't persuaded you to talk to him again you would have gone and we would have carried on as before.

DANILO. That's exactly what is going to happen.

[*She shakes her head. Pause.*]

LYDIA. It won't ever be the same...Dimetos, Sophia, and myself
Something has happened.

DANILO. What?

LYDIA. I don't know...but it's suddenly like we've all got secret
from each other.

DANILO. That's bad. And I'm the cause.

LYDIA. I wish you were. I wish there was just one person or thin
to blame. But I know you aren't...not in that way.
I'm not making sense.

DANILO. You sure you are not just depressed because...well, th
possibility of getting away from here seems to have been lost?

LYDIA [*with absolute sincerity*]. I'd give up any chance of ever goin
back to the city if the three of us could go back to what it wa
like...five days ago. It's changed so suddenly!
There's an old man who lives at the bottom of the road pa
our house. I use to think he was mad because no matter what
would say to him, he just shrugged his shoulders and answere
'Tomorrow was yesterday.' I know what he means now, and
wish it was true.

DANILO [*Shaking his head angrily*]. No! That is not good enough.

LYDIA. I'd be happy if it was true.

DANILO. Don't say that! You've let them frighten you. Don't argu
with me. Answer me honestly...are you frightened?

LYDIA. Yes.

[*The admission leaves Danilo almost speechless.*]

DANILO [*quietly, sincerely*]. Leave them, Lydia. No...you listen t
me now. When the time comes, and it can't be far off...you leav
them. Even if you were his daughter I'd say as much.

LYDIA. No.

DANILO. All you owe him is gratitude, and you've obviously pai
that debt in full. You don't owe him your life. No! I haven
finished. I want to tell you about an old man *I* know. Strange
enough he also lives at the bottom of a road. In a funny littl
house made of 'real bricks'. A little boy carries out a chair fir
thing in the morning, puts it down on the pavement...and a litt
later the old man comes slowly out, sits down and watches—th
people passing on the pavement, the traffic in the street, encounte
between friends, arguments between neighbours, accidents .

Life! He'd been watching it for a long time when finally one day
I plucked up enough courage to stop and talk to him. I wasn't
much older than you and...I had a question. 'Excuse me, sir',
I said, 'But can you help me...' [*Pause.*] Before I could go any
further he shook his head sadly and said 'No. I'm too old. Help
yourself.'

LYDIA [*laughing*]. You've just made that up.

DANILO. That's right. Don't you think it was good?

LYDIA. Until you couldn't think of a question to ask him.

DANILO. Can you?

LYDIA. Why is nothing forever?

DANILO [*shaking his head*]. No. You want to feel sorry for yourself.
Forever? What does that mean? Museums try to make things
'forever'. Do you want to do that to yourself? Stick a pin through
your 'five days ago' and still be there in a hundred years of time?
You've lost faith in tomorrow Lydia...and I'm going to give it
back to you.

LYDIA. How?

DANILO. Oh, God, I wish I knew.
[*He kisses her gently. At first Lydia responds but as Danilo goes
further she begins to resist him. He can't control himself. The struggle
becomes violent. Her dress gets torn. She eventually manages to break
free and runs away. Danilo is left alone.*]
Danilo? Danilo?

Scene 10

Lydia, *her dress torn, alone.* Sophia *enters.*

SOPHIA [*terrified of her question and its possible answer, but unable to
resist asking it*]. Who ... who was it?
I saw a most beautiful bird.
Lydia who was it?
I saw a marvellous dragonfly ...
Lydia please ... Who was it?
Remember our funny little chicken ...
Lydia, who was it!

I saw a pretty little blue egg . . .
[*Sinking to her knees beside Lydia.*] Lydia, please help me. Who
was it? [*Her pain turns to violence. She scrambles to her feet and
assaults Lydia physically.*] For God's sake, tell me. Who was it?

LYDIA. Danilo.
[*Pause.*]

SOPHIA. Danilo. [*She starts laughing, finally uncontrollably.*] Don't let
it upset you too much. A pretty little thing like you will have to
cope with a lot more passion before she's old. But in your prayers
tonight make sure you ask that it be the other person's and not
your own. To love is a position of weakness, to be loved a position
of power. I was careless about my prayers when I was your age.
[*Pause.*] I did warn you. Now I'm going to leave you. [*Exit.*]

Scene 11

Lydia, *alone and very frightened.* Dimetos *enters. He is breathless,
his manner wild and disturbed. He is frightened of his hands.*

DIMETOS. Did he . . . hurt you? There . . . there . . . it's . . . it's all over
now. And so, very nearly, is today. You must go to bed . . . sleep
. . . and when you wake up . . . all that happened will already be
yesterday. Time is not always our enemy, Lydia. What shall we
do tomorrow? You decide. Something . . . something impossible.
My hands want to work.

LYDIA. Your hands smell of lemons. You were the man in the orchard.
You were watching us. You didn't stop him.
[*Pause.*]

DIMETOS. You ran away before I needed to. I wouldn't have let him
hurt you. [*Looking at his hands.*] It was so hot. The blossom made
me giddy. I remember holding onto a branch . . . I must have
crushed the leaves. Do you know what day this is? The solstice.
The longest day of the year. This was the longest day of the year.
From *sol*, meaning sun, and *sistere,* to stand still. The day the
sun stood still. So did I. I never knew I had that much stillness
in me. Only my shadow moved. And then at a moment, together
with the sun, that seemed to stop as well. I thought I was going to
faint. You were so long in coming. I closed my eyes, and then

36

as if I was dreaming, I saw you again beside the well waiting to go down, modest and beautiful. I saw you on the horse and then afterwards in the pool. I heard your laugh again ... but that wasn't my dream. I opened my eyes and there you were. He kissed you. [*Pause.*] This will be the shortest night. The year has turned on its side. We've so much time left Lydia. Don't be frightened. We'll save all the stray horses that fall into wells.

LYDIA [*quietly*]. Go.

[*Exit Dimetos. Lydia is alone.*]

I know your story now. You didn't know that men make holes in the world. You thought it was safe. So you trusted it. Grass is green ... water is sweet ... the shade of big trees is cool ... and you walked and galloped as if it was all there just for you. But one day, without any warning ... down, down, down to the bottom where it was cold and dark and you were alone and you were frightened. Horses are stupid. Stupid, stupid horses. Stray and fall. For all its holes the world is still worth it—because Dimetos makes happy endings. [*She climbs on to the table, pulls down a rope hanging from the ceiling. Speaking with authority.*] We need a knot that won't slip. The rope must bite into itself and tighten when subjected to strain. I can do it with my eyes closed. [*She ties the knot, puts the noose around her neck, and hangs herself.*]

ACT TWO

Scene 1

Beside the Ocean. Many years later. Dimetos, *older, on the beach.*

DIMETOS. Sea. Sand. Sun. Sky. Elemental. There could be a beginning here, as easily as an end. The footprints leading across the wet sand to this moment, suggest a purpose.

The tide has pulled out so far I despair of its return. The sand underfoot is loose and heavy and when I try to ease the weight of my emptiness with handfulls of it, it spills out between my fingers as if my fists were lunatic hour-glasses, impatient to measure out what's left of my time. There are no landmarks. You walk until you've had enough.

Scene 2

A small cottage. Dimetos *and* Sophia *at a window.*

SOPHIA. What is it?

DIMETOS. I'm not sure. I can't get close enough. It looks like one of the Cetaceans.

SOPHIA. Speak English.

DIMETOS. One of the sea mammals . . . maybe a walrus. It was very frustrating. That rock is so close. But even with the tide as low as it is, I couldn't reach it.

SOPHIA. Why did you throw stones?

DIMETOS. To see if it was dead.

SOPHIA. Is it?

DIMETOS. I think so. It didn't move. Must have crawled onto that rock during the night and died. It wasn't there yesterday. I wouldn't have noticed it if it wasn't for a bad smell on the way

38

back. At first I thought it was something in one of the pools. Then
I saw the gulls.

SOPHIA. Your stones disturbed them.

DIMETOS. I know. Didn't take them long to settle down again though,
did it? There's a good meal for them there.

SOPHIA. I see.

DIMETOS [*moving away from the window*]. Yes...they're essentially
scavengers.

SOPHIA. Just lie there and rot. It's going to stink.

DIMETOS. Unfortunately yes. When the wind turns we will know all
about it.

[*He empties his pockets of a collection of stones and shells onto a
small table already cluttered with similar debris. Sophia leaves the
window.*]

SOPHIA. A good walk?

DIMETOS. Yes. Almost too pleasant. I'm getting a little tired of this
perfect weather now. It's beginning to feel as if there is nothing
left to happen except a blue sky and calm water. I don't think
I've ever seen the sea so still in the...time we've been here.

SOPHIA. Here? This one? Three years now.

DIMETOS. You say that as if you've counted the days.

SOPHIA. Not deliberately.

DIMETOS. Three years. As long as that.

SOPHIA. Is it time to move again?

DIMETOS. I don't think so.

SOPHIA. That's good. Because I don't know what you would do if
it was. We can't go any further, you know. This is the limit. There
is nowhere from here except back.

DIMETOS. I'm content here. Aren't you?

SOPHIA [*She is staring at him.*] What do you shout at the sea? You
were standing at the edge of the water, looking out over the waves.
You put your hands to your mouth and shouted something. I
couldn't hear.

DIMETOS. Oh that! Just a game. The little waves were lively, full of
surprise. Almost as if the sea wanted to play. I thought maybe
that *that* innocence was still possible. So I threw it my name.
The waves will break it up and tomorrow, after high tide, I'll
pick up the pieces.

39

SOPHIA. So that is what they are.

DIMETOS. The pieces of my name.

SOPHIA. Is the sea obliging, Dimetos? Does it always let you win
As a little boy you would never play if there was a chance o
losing.

DIMETOS. It's not one of those games. There's no winning or losing
We play just for the fun of it.

SOPHIA. Throwing stones and playing games. You know what tha
sounds like, don't you? Dimetos's hands have come to an end
That's a lament worthy of a poet. It was strange seeing you so
helpless you had to resort to throwing a stone. For a moment
almost saw the little boy I was led to a long time ago. Do yo
remember? 'Dimetos, this is Sophia. She will look after you.'

DIMETOS [*holding up a round beach-rolled stone*]. Look, nearly perfect
I couldn't do better if I tried. And this almost perfect shape i
without a purpose. Form without a function. The sea is a cleve
but mad craftsman, Sophia. His is the ultimate mockery. Yo
should relax. He ridicules my hands and all they did more than
you ever will. A colossal and totally absurd energy. I imagin
there is more in one tide pushing up that beach than a man use
in a life-time. The energy in one wave could build a wall. Bu
what does it do instead? . . . polish stones until they disappear.

SOPHIA. It also makes you skip sometimes. You never tell me abou
the waves you don't see coming. Preserving your dignity? On
caught you this afternoon. [*She laughs.*]

DIMETOS. Yes, one did. You watch me very carefully, Sophia, don'
you?

SOPHIA. Yes.

DIMETOS. Are you frightened I might leave you?

SOPHIA. Yes. I'm frightened of that. Have you ever tried?

DIMETOS. No.

SOPHIA. I find that hard to believe.

DIMETOS. Do you? In all the years since . . . Have I ever walked to
fast for you?

SOPHIA. No, you haven't. But why. You must have surely though
about it.

DIMETOS. Not even that. I have no argument left, Sophia . . . least o
all with my fate.

SOPHIA. So I've finally got an identity. Not mother, sister, companion or friend . . . but your fate.

DIMETOS. Part of it.

SOPHIA. Not all?

DIMETOS. No. You'ld like to be though, wouldn't you?

SOPHIA. I'll tell you something you don't know. I've tried to leave you, and not just thought about it. Physically started walking away. Several times. You never noticed because no attempt lasted very long and do you know why? The thought of you alive— seeing, hearing, doing, and eventually forgetting . . . without me, the thought that there might be even just one moment's happiness for you, without me—was a hell I couldn't endure. [*She goes to the window.*] The wind has turned. You're right. I can smell it now. [*As she leaves the room*] Your socks must be wet. Take them off.

Scene 3

Danilo. *Like* Dimetos *and* Sophia, *he has aged*.

DANILO. And that is more or less how it was when I found him again. A sense of it all being over . . . all the adventures and mis-adventures finally parcelled up and packed away to gather dust . . . which of course was true for all of us. He was down on the beach, staring vacantly out to sea. There's a sense of retribution in the image, isn't there? Behind him land and a world of men he would never return to, who didn't want him any more, had in fact finally forgotten him. And ahead of him the ocean, a world he could not enter . . . unless he was tempted to act out a fanciful metaphor for the last adventure of all. That didn't appear to be likely, however. To all intents and purposes he had come to terms with himself in that no-man's land between the tides, collecting his sea shells. If there was something more at work I saw no evidence of it.

Scene 4

Danilo *finds* Dimetos *on the beach.*

DANILO [*calling*]. Dimetos! You've forgotten!

DIMETOS. No, I haven't! Danilo!

DANILO. That's right! You're not surprised to see me?

DIMETOS. No. I half-expected you to try and find me again!
[*They meet.*]

DANILO. It was hard enough the first time. This time it was almost
impossible. You have a talent, Dimetos, for the remote and inaccessible.

DIMETOS. And you for proving they are not that.

DANILO. Did you move here directly?

DIMETOS. No. We wandered around for quite a long time, before
ending up here.

DANILO. You covered your tracks very well.

DIMETOS. Not deliberately. Word of what had happened spread.
Nobody would have anything to do with us.

DANILO [*A deep breath of the sea air.*] It's at least healthy here.

DIMETOS. And quiet.

DANILO. Yes. I hardly passed a soul on the last day's travelling.

DIMETOS. A few fishermen come this way occasionally.

DANILO. It is as I expected.
I've never forgotten the feeling I had, when I found you in that
village, of having travelled back in time. Heaven knows that was
primitive enough... but this!

DIMEOTS. Shell-grit. That little bay has a rocky bottom. Waves and
tides have reduced the shells to this. I sell it inland to the farmers.
They feed it to their poultry.

DANILO. A very basic operation.

DIMETOS. Yes. My last apprenticeship, Danilo. To the sea. My
Master's only tool is time.
[*He works. Danilo watches him.*]

DANILO. Are you alone?

DIMETOS. Haven't you seen Sophia?

DANILO. No. At the cottage?

DIMETOS. Yes.

DANILO. She must have been out. I knocked and called but no one answered.
[*They walk.*]

DIMETOS. And the city?

DANILO. In trouble as usual. But I'm resigned to that now. Crisis is obviously its permanent environment.

DIMETOS. You had vision once, Danilo.

DANILO. Don't embarrass me. Vision. No, Dimetos. A few old cranks and their young followers still keep that word alive. The rest of us muddle along as best we can. I came across a theory the other day which struck a responsive chord. The City of the Living—our metropolis—has its origins in the City of the Dead—the necropolis. That is how it all started, apparently, with burial grounds...a permanent place not for the living, but the dead. Sometimes I think it's on its way back to being that. But tell me more about yourself. I suppose you left the village immediately after...

DIMETOS. Yes.

DANILO. I didn't imagine you would stay on.

DIMETOS. Superstition gained the upper hand. They feared bad crops. Threatened to stone us. They wouldn't let me bury her there.

DANILO. So what did you do?

DIMETOS. Nothing. We just...left...What have you come for this time, Danilo?

DANILO. To see you.

DIMETOS. About what?

DANILO. Nothing. I literally meant...just see you. When I got back to the city and time passed without any news of you reaching us, I assumed something had happened, that you were dead. It came as quite a shock to hear that you were in fact still alive. Because you see, Dimetos, I eventually worked out what had really happened during those five days with you. You do understand, don't you, that her death was on *my* conscience. She committed suicide because of what *I* had done. When I eventually realized that it belonged on yours...! [*Pause.*] You had a guilty love for her didn't you? When I discovered that, everything fell into place. The endless flow of wine; the frequency with which I found myself, as I thought, alone with her. Because you were watching all the time. All your sober and serious thinking about returning to the city was just a ploy to keep me on.

Those five days must rank as one of your more ingenious pieces of engineering. You used us like tools and with such consummate mastery because of your passion for your niece. She was your only real mistake . . . a miscalculation of the stress that little soul could take. So there it was. Dimetos's last piece of ingenuity. I'm sorry to rake up the past like this, but do you know what it did to me? I went back to the city, my life, despising myself. Because of that I started despising others. When I eventually stumbled on your responsibility for all that happened, and realized that mine was that measure smaller . . . it was too late. I despised myself more . . . to the extent that when I heard you were alive I couldn't even think of revenging myself for what you had done. I am here simply out of morbid curiosity to see what you had also done to yourself.

DIMETOS. What have you found, Danilo?

DANILO. Dimetos older, quieter, but tanned and healthy. Looking at you it would seem as if your actions have run dry of consequences in your life. Because you did know what you were doing, didn't you?

DIMETOS. Yes.

DANILO. And you did try to stop yourself?

DIMETOS. Yes.

DANILO. So did I. Why couldn't we? This rational intelligence of ours, our special human capacity for anticipating, predicting pain . . . our own or another's . . . as the consequence of an action, was useless, wasn't it?

DIMETOS. What are you trying to say, Danilo? What do you want?

DANILO. Punishment. Not just for you specifically, but as a fundamental law of the universe, and of a magnitude on a par with your gravity. Because without it our notions of justice man-made or natural, of good and evil, are the most pathetic illusions we have ever entertained. Maybe I came too soon. After all, you're still alive. Who knows? Who knows anything? [*Danilo goes.*]

[*Dimetos alone.*]

DIMETOS. Tide's turning. Mustn't get my feet wet again.

'. . . That flowing and swelling of the sea, or its alternate rising and falling, twice in each lunar day, due to the attraction of the moon and to a lesser degree of the sun . . . the space of time between two successive points of High Water . . .'

Scene 5

The cottage. Dimetos *and* Sophia.

SOPHIA. Who was the man on the beach?

DIMETOS. Didn't you recognize him?

SOPHIA. Danilo.

DIMETOS. Yes. Where were you?

SOPHIA. Here.

DIMETOS. You didn't answer when he knocked.

SOPHIA. There are no doors left to open . . . least of all to him. What did he want?

DIMETOS. We talked about . . . the past.

SOPHIA. My God, are we still frightened of her name. So you talked about 'the past'. Did you finally confess to him?

DIMETOS. I didn't have to.

SOPHIA. He knew, did he. Had he worked it out?

DIMETOS. Yes.

SOPHIA. Everything.

DIMETOS. Just about.

SOPHIA. What did he say about me?

DIMETOS. Nothing.

SOPHIA. What did you tell him?

DIMETOS. About you? Nothing.

SOPHIA. I wasn't important, was I? Yours is unquestionably the most selfish soul I have ever known. Your life, your passion and now *your* guilt. You want to take all of that as well don't you? [*Confronting him.*] You understand nothing. She could have been my child, you know. We were the right ages. When she first came to us I was frightened of her . . . I don't know why, but I was more frightened of her than I had been of anything before, or since. One day I found her alone, somewhere . . . her room I think . . . and I just knew, just realized that she was also frightened of me. An

45

impulse made me tell her. When I did we just laughed, and laughed . . . and at the end of it we had adopted each other.

Do you know how to go to heaven? We worked out a way. Ten beautiful . . .

[*She speaks with sombre passion.*]

No, Dimetos. NO! She would still be alive today if I hadn't abandoned her to . . . You are not God! If I had so much as put my arm around her when she sat there wilting . . . one gentle touch and I had it in my soul. But I was jealous and I knew, that left to your own devices, you were going to hurt her. So I went for a walk, for a long walk. [*Pause.*] A long time ago I committed myself to your life. That was a mistake, and in making it I wrecked mine utterly. That knowledge is all I'm left with. You are not going to take that away.

[*She goes to the window.*] It's really starting to stink now. Good night. [*She goes.*]

[*Dimetos is alone.*]

DIMETOS. Tides . . . tides . . .

Let E and M be the centres of the earth and moon respectively; let R be the radius of the earth which will be assumed to be a sphere. Let ME and MM be the centres of the earth and the moon respectively. Expressed in the same units . . . Lydia . . .

. . . the attractive force of the earth on a unit mass on its surface is G, where G is the force of Gravity on the earth's surface . . . Lydia . . .

. . . since the attractive force varies directly as the mass and inversely as the square of the distance . . . Lydia . . .

. . . since the attractive force varies directly as the mass and inversely as the square of the distance . . . Lydia . . .

. . . at new and full moons when these times and tides coincide, the crest would be under the moon, and at the quadrature, the solar wave crest and trough combining symmetrically with the lunar wave crest and trough respectively, produce merely a difference in height and not in displacement . . . LYDIA! [*Pause.*]

Don't look, Dimetos. Don't look.

Lydia . . . The silence chokes on your name, as if that knot will never let another sound into the world. I am going to try to let you down. That won't be easy . . . because there is no measure to the distance between your feet and the earth they never reached.

But I've got hands ... all I need to do ... is use them ...

Scene 6

Dimetos *and* Sophia. Sophia *holds a handkerchief to her nose.*
Dimetos *is at the table fiddling compulsively with his beach debris.*

SOPHIA. All the windows are closed but that only seems to have made
it worse. It's trapped in here now. The smell of decay has itself
started to decay. [*She is at the window. She laughs.*] The birds are
so gorged they can't leave that rock. The wind is bowling them
off it like ten-pins. There goes another one! [*She prowls.*] You
said it wouldn't last long.

DIMETOS. It's only been blowing for three days.

SOPHIA. And done nothing but get stronger.

DIMETOS. Once it's reached its peak it will start to abate.

SOPHIA. That better be soon. I can't stand it much longer.

DIMETOS. If you find it so intolerable ...

SOPHIA. Don't you!

DIMETOS [*trying to ignore the interruption*]. .... if you find it so intolerable go away until it's all over.

SOPHIA. Go away.

DIMETOS. You're free to do so.

SOPHIA. Very clever, Dimetos. If I didn't know otherwise I could
believe that you'd hauled that bloody thing onto the rock deliberately. Stink her out! You'd try anything, wouldn't you? No.
You won't get rid of me that easily. [*Watching him.*] And if you
want to do something with your hands why don't you try hauling
it off. You've done nothing but fidget and fiddle for days. A rotting
carcass can't surely defeat a great engineer.

DIMETOS. Stop it, Sophia!

SOPHIA. Or put them in your pockets since your toys don't make
them happy any more. That's what naughty boys do. I had to
smack yours once or twice for that, remember? Is that when you
fell in love with your hands?

[*He ignores her. She sits down at her end of the table, where*

47

there is a small heap of lemon leaves. She starts crushing them in her hands and smelling them.]

These are the last few left. I've stripped the tree bare. Didn' help anyway ... or if anything only made it worse ... like making filth palatable. It's permeating everything ... even thinking make me want to vomit. What should we try next? Go for a nice long walk, Dimetos, and find us a sweet-smelling herb native to these parts to spice the prevailing odour of death and decay. You haven't been out for days.

DIMETOS. The weather outside is not very inviting ...

SOPHIA [*cutting him*]. Nor for that matter the weather inside! First time I've known that to stop you though. I thought you liked your playmate in his unruly moods. You should see him. He' throwing everything around on that beach except ... A moment' respite from you would also be a relief. I used to enjoy watching your hands work, but their present idiocy is driving me mad What are you trying to do!

DIMETOS. [*His compulsive fiddling with his shells and stones has now become obsessive. His hands seem to have a life of their own.* Nothing ... just ...

SOPHIA. Playing another game.

DIMETOS. Yes. It's like a puzzle. I can't believe that these don' somehow ... fit together ... that a human intelligence can't make sense of them ...

SOPHIA. But they do?

DIMETOS [*desperate innocence*]. They do ...?

SOPHIA. Yes ... your name. Don't you remember. They spel D-I-M-E-T-O-S ...

DIMETOS. NO.

SOPHIA. What's the matter?

DIMETOS. Nothing.

SOPHIA. What was that thought? [*Dimetos shakes his head. Sophia watching him carefully.*] I'll find out ... unless this wind doesn turn and we die of suffocation.

What an end. They survived their own consciences and othe men's stoning, but were suffocated to death by the stench of carcass. [*Violently.*] Don't you also smell the damned thing!

DIMETOS. Stop talking about it!

SOPHIA. Silence only makes it worse. I refuse to surrender to it. You know something... sometimes it seems as if you are doing more than just endure it... that you refuse to admit it's there.

DIMETOS. When the wind turns...

SOPHIA [*hysterically*]. There's a rotten carcass on that rock, Dimetos!

DIMETOS. Sophia!

SOPHIA. Then tell me what's in your mind!

[*Dimetos is too exhausted, too desperate, to put up any further defence.*]

DIMETOS. A dream...

SOPHIA. When?

DIMETOS. The night before last.

SOPHIA. The day Danilo was here.

DIMETOS. Yes.

SOPHIA. What happened?

DIMETOS. I can't remember.

SOPHIA. Try.

DIMETOS. I have. I woke up with my hands... desperate... they had to do something... but it eludes me. There are moments when I seem on the point of remembering...

SOPHIA. I'll help you.

DIMETOS [*frightened*]. No.

[*Pause... Sophia and Dimetos look at each other in their separate and private desperations.*]

SOPHIA. It's... Lydia... isn't it?

DIMETOS. She's still hanging there. I can't get her down. Time is passing, Sophia...

SOPHIA. That's what is really stinking in this room. She messed herself when she reached the end of that rope. I had to clean her. [*She goes to the window.*] Lydia. [*Pause.*] There is a woman... somewhere, sitting... immobile but not frozen... she will move again. Warm and beautiful, but one eye, her head is turned in profile... is fixed on something evil, ugly... like a hawk's eye. I found her... at the end of a long walk... which I had taken to put a lot of distance between myself and something I was afraid of... something inevitable. It wasn't easy. As I walked the day changed... the sun bleached all colour out of the world... places and things which I passed, and knew, were strange and ugly. But I

kept on ... because I had an appointment. My sense of it was so
strong I started to run. The road got stonier and stonier. I reached
the pool. The water was dark, and turgid. The day was night.
That is where I found her ... sitting, waiting for me ... her knees
drawn up under her chin. Her feet are misshapen ... her hair, long
and soft, lies gently around her face. But it's all a lie. There is
something wrong with her. She keeps company with a donkey, an
owl, a griffin, a bat and an old, million-year-old turtle. There is a
terrible familiarity between herself and the entrance to hell, which
is just behind her. She goes in and out. She was waiting for me.
If I could tell you ... If you could help me ... I loved Dimetos.

[*She leaves the window and goes to him. He no longer registers her
presence. She puts out a hand and touches him gently and then laughs
for the second time. At the end of it she leaves him. Dimetos is alone.*]

DIMETOS. Time is passing ... nowhere to nowhere ... Time is at
work ... [*Pause.*] Work ... Work!

The effect produced in any mass by a force acting against inertia
or resistance ... an effect that may merely result in strain or
produce motion of the mass ... the rate of work is power ... because
power takes account of time ... Force, work, power!

Apply them ... [*Using his beach debris he goes to work.*] ... make a
tool, a machine that will stop time ...

Machine, a primary machine.

The lever! First order. Fulcrum between force and weight ...
crowbar, pumphandle ...

[*It doesn't stop time.*]

No. Second order. Weight between fulcrum and force ... wheel-
barrow, nutcracker ...

[*It also doesn't stop time.*]

No. Third order. Force between weight and fulcrum ... treadle
of a lathe, sugar tongs, forearm ... No. Still passing ... moving ...
Motion! Every body will maintain its state of rest or of uniform
motion in a straight line unless compelled by some external force
to change that state and this rate of change is directly proportional
to the force ...

... to every action there is an equal and opposite reaction ...

... because every particle of matter in the universe attracts
every other particle with a force whose direction is that of the line
joining the two and whose magnitude is directly as the product

of the masses and inversely as the square of the distance from each other ... Time stinks. Time stinks! [*He is totally defeated.*] What must I do?

LYDIA's VOICE. Keep calm. Don't be frightened. Can you hear me clearly?

DIMETOS. Yes.

VOICE. Your hands. Find your hands. Look at them. They are useless. The only tool a man can make that will help him hold time, is a story. The theory is very simple: adapting the principle of a lever of the first order we will place in exact opposition, on a common pivot, the clean edges of a beginning, and an end. The beginning, Dimetos. Make a beginning ...

DIMETOS. Beginning ... 'The point at which anything starts or commences ... ' Once upon a time ...

VOICE. Now the end.

DIMETOS. For ever after.

VOICE. And now the pivot.

DIMETOS. Pivot ... 'That on which anything turns or depends ... the cardinal, central or vital point ... ' There was.

VOICE. Now put them together.

DIMETOS. Once upon a time ... there was ... for ever after. Once upon a time ... there was ... for ever after.

[*He begins to play with the words ... repetition of them all in sequence and individual elements. From a clumsy, awkward start we see a facility develop. He tries every concievable variation. At the end he is handling them with the facility of a consumate story-teller.*]

VOICE. You've made your tool, Dimetos. Now comes the hard part. Use it.

DIMETOS. Once upon a time, there was ... a man ... who dreamt he was a horse. He had fallen out of the world into a place where it was cold and dark and he was frightened. And because he was an animal that fear lasted for ever. There was no hoping or waiting for help, just successive eternities of cold mud, the darkness in his very open eyes, and nowhere to go. He tried, but there was nowhere else to go.

And so, it was from nowhere that she came. And from her first sound and touch, to the last heavy loss of her weight when she went back to nowhere, he trusted her. He wasn't alone.

They pulled him up. He galloped away. And the place where he had been, the thing that had happened to him, also went back to nowhere. But that night under a tree, with the world around him once again the way it was when he first found it, he remembered her and wanted her. And because of this, his desire to possess her was so great that that night he dreamt his hooves turned into hands. Because of this he had to stand very still, hold on to the grass very tight, because he couldn't walk. The danger of falling again was very real. Another eternity of fear followed until she came a second time, from nowhere, and was on his back again. She was laughing and he understood from that, that she wanted him to gallop away with her into the world. But he couldn't move. His hooves were hands. He was frightened of falling. So she left him.

And because of this his torment was so great that that night, he dreamt he was a man. He could walk. His hands were free. He could work. And because he was a man he could hope now and wait. And while he was hoping and waiting he put his hands to work making a world for her so that he could hear her laugh again the way she had when he was a horse. Eternities of making and working passed while he waited and hoped. He mastered the four elements of the universe. He disciplined water in pipes, air in bellows, fire in furnaces and the earth he shaped with the extravagance of a profligate. But she never came.

And because of this, his despair was so great that that night he dreamt his hands without himself. A voice was talking to them:

'All you ever wanted to do was possess. All you've ever made were tools and machines to help you do that. It is now time for the skills you scorned. Find something and hold it. Close that powerful hand on a thing. Yours. Hold it! The act of defiance man has made his creed. The mortal human hold! Now give it away. Don't be frightened. Only to your other hand. It will still be yours. That's right. Hold it. Tight. That was a terrible second when they were both empty. One still is. Find something. Quickly! Now comes the hard part . . . so listen carefully. Each must give what it has got to the other, at the same time. You must give and take with the same action.

Again . . . and again . . .

[*Dimetos's hands juggle. He starts to laugh . . . and laughs and*

laughs.]
  And now, because your gaiety is so great, the last skill of all.
  Hold them out, and wait . . .

CURTAIN

NONGOGO

Act I—Queeny's shebeen in Johannesburg
Act II—The next morning
Act III—Late that afternoon

CHARACTERS

JOHNNY	a young African salesman
QUEENY	a shebeen proprietress
BLACKIE	a hanger-on
SAM	a friend of Queeny's
PATRICK	one of her customers

This play was given its first performance outside South Africa on 27 November 1974 at the Crucible Studio, Sheffield, with the following cast directed by Peter James:

Johnny	*Jimi Rand*
Queeny	*Ena Cabayo*
Sam	*Alton Kumalo*
Patrick	*Nik Abraham*

Nongogo: a woman for two-and-six, a term especially used of prostitutes soliciting amongst the lines of gold-mine workers queuing for their pay.

ACT ONE

Queeny's shebeen in one of the townships around Johannesburg. The time is late Friday afternoon. The room is small, with two doors— one at the back leading onto the street, the other on the o.p. side leading into a kitchen, which is not seen. There is one window looking onto the street.

The furniture includes a divan at the back which is curtained off to suggest an alcove. There are also a table, chairs, a sideboard, and a dressing table. The furniture is expensive by township standards but nevertheless there is a suggestion of slovenliness about the room. The window curtains, for example, are nondescript, while those separating the divan from the rest of the room have a few rings missing and hang askew. There is no order or pattern to the ornaments and oddments in the room. Odd articles of female clothing are scattered about.

As the scene opens the room appears empty; the curtains surrounding the divan are drawn. Street noises are heard from outside. Then some one knocks at the door and gets no answer. The door, pushed lightly from outside, swings open and Johnny *comes in. He is a young man, neatly but quietly dressed. An open collar and loose tie suggest a hot day. He is carrying a suitcase. He looks around, sees nobody, and is just about to leave when something about the room attracts his attention. He comes back and looks at the table, runs a finger along it, and whistles approvingly. He is examining the sideboard when one of the curtains round the divan is drawn back roughly and* Queeny *sticks out her head. She is in her forties; a woman of powerful personality; what must have been tremendous beauty in her youth now shows the signs of age. She is a personification of the room: the very best but neglected.*

QUEENY [*rudely*]. What do you want?

JOHNNY. Sorry ... The door was open and ...

QUEENY. And you just walked in!

JOHNNY. Yes...But I did knock.

QUEENY. Okay. Now walk out just as quietly. I only start selling at seven.

JOHNNY [*bewildered*]. Selling?

QUEENY. You heard me. Seven. Either stay thirsty until then or find some other place...There's enough of them.

JOHNNY [*recognizing the room*]. I see. A shebeen.

QUEENY. I said seven o'clock.

JOHNNY. I don't want a drink.

QUEENY. Get out!

JOHNNY [*trying to calm her down*]. Look...Let me explain...

QUEENY [*going to the window and calling into the street*]. Blackie! Blackie!

JOHNNY. Who's Blackie?

QUEENY. You'll find out.

JOHNNY [*bending down to his suitcase*]. All I wanted...

[*He gets no further. The door opens and* Blackie *comes in. An ugly hunchback, about twenty-three, his arms hang loose at his sides like those of a large ape.*]

BLACKIE. What's the matter?

QUEENY [*points at Johnny and then turns her back*]. Him!

JOHNNY [*retreating before the menacing figure of Blackie who comes towards him*]. I didn't know this was a shebeen...and I don't drink...All I wanted to do is try and sell you a table cloth.

QUEENY [*astonished*]. A what?

JOHNNY. A table cloth. I sell table cloths.

QUEENY [*suspicious*]. Are you fooling?

BLACKIE [*threatening*]. Get out.

[*Johnny turns to Queeny imploringly. Blackie hesitates. Queeny pauses for a second, looks carefully at Johnny, then gestures to Blackie to leave.*]

BLACKIE [*pausing at the door and looking suspiciously at Johnny*]. I'll be outside. [*He exits.*]

JOHNNY. What was that?

QUEENY. A friend.

JOHNNY [*incredulous*]. A friend...You mean a watchdog. Just like

60

the whites. Only you don't have a notice on your door.

QUEENY. You shouldn't frighten people.

JOHNNY. Frighten?

QUEENY. Coming in here like you was up to no good.

JOHNNY [*shaking his head*]. Me?... Frightening people... up to no good? All I do is sell table cloths. Which reminds me... It's not a very big range, only red and blue, but the colours don't run.

QUEENY. What do I want with a table cloth?

JOHNNY. For your table. Look, that's good wood. [*He examines the table closely.*]... And here, see! Stains! I say, it's essential for a respectable shebeen with a good table like this to have one of my table cloths.

[*Queeny has been watching him carefully. She starts smiling and at the end of his little sales talk bursts into laughter. Her personality changes... the moody aggressive person is gone.*]

JOHNNY [*responding immediately*]. You don't laugh very often, do you?

QUEENY [*stopping abruptly*]. Why do you say that?

JOHNNY. I never expected it.

QUEENY. [*The aggression returns.*] Why don't you go sell your table cloths?

JOHNNY [*wearily*]. *Ja*, I suppose I'd better. Where's the best part to try?

QUEENY. You mean has anybody got any money? [*Johnny nods.*] Nobody's got any money over here.

JOHNNY. Except you... and you got it all.

QUEENY. Look...

JOHNNY. It's true, isn't it?

QUEENY. Better watch your tongue if you want to stay out of trouble.

JOHNNY. I'm always getting that advice... and quite often the trouble. But I can't help it. It's what you see that starts you talking and I see just the same as other folks, don't I? [*Gesturing towards the room.*] But then maybe I don't... Like your laugh. Maybe other people never seen that.

QUEENY [*turning away*]. Maybe not. [*Pause.*] No, not many people have seen that.

JOHNNY. You should show it off. It's good. [*Queeny turns and looks at Johnny. It is a split second of emberrassment. Johnny picks up his suitcase.*] Anyway...

QUEENY. Look, maybe I like the way you speak. Have a drink on the house.

JOHNNY. I don't drink.

QUEENY. Cup of coffee?

JOHNNY. Thanks... but I'd better try selling or I won't be able to buy myself one tonight.

QUEENY. That's right... I forgot. You sell table cloths. You know maybe I do need one after all.

JOHNNY [*hopefully*]. You think so?

QUEENY. *Ja*, a blue one.

JOHNNY. No!

QUEENY. What do you mean no?

JOHNNY. The red one.

QUEENY [*bewildered*]. The red one?

JOHNNY. Yes. It suits this room much better.

QUEENY. You think so?

JOHNNY [*enthusiastic*]. Of course. It's a good strong colour... matches you. These things go together, you know. [*Explaining* Look, if you were buying a scarf or something you'd match it wouldn't you... see that it goes with your best dress or something like that. [*Queeny nods in agreement*.] Well same thing in the house, and this red is your colour.

QUEENY. All right, a red one. How much?

JOHNNY. Five bob.

QUEENY. There.

JOHNNY. My first sale today.

QUEENY. Maybe you'll sell four in the next street.

JOHNNY. Maybe. Anyway, thanks.

QUEENY. Okay... Now don't go frightening people or you won't se any. [*She is trying to delay his departure*.] Hey look... when yo finish tonight come around and have that cup of coffee.

JOHNNY. Don't know if I can. I gotta catch the bus back to Alex.

QUEENY. Tomorrow?

JOHNNY. I won't be back after tonight. Looks like nobody war table cloths except you. Anyway, thanks.

[*Johnny exits. Queeny looks blankly at the door that has closed in h face. She is alone. She is alone again. She sits down on the div takes out a cigarette, lights it, and puffs away thoughtfully for a few minutes. Then she gets up and goes across to the mirror and examines her face carefully, running a finger over a few lines. She stubs out her cigarette in disgust and returns to the divan, only to light another and surrender herself to the boredom which Johnny's entrance and exit have now highlighted. The door opens and Blackie comes in. He stands there, looking at her, waiting for a word. He gets none. He hobbles a little closer.*]

BLACKIE. He's gone. [*Queeny nods her head.*] I saw him go down the street. [*Pause.*] I followed him a little way to make sure he wasn't coming back.

QUEENY [*sharply*]. I told you to leave him alone.

BLACKIE [*hurt*]. You said nothing.

QUEENY [*irritable*]. Well I'm telling you now.

BLACKIE [*sees the red table cloth and picks it up*]. Why'd you buy this?

QUEENY [*jumps up and takes it away from him*]. Because I wanted it. that's why.

BLACKIE [*trying to please*]. I can get you better.

QUEENY. I wanted this one. It matches the room.

BLACKIE. He said that.

QUEENY [*angry*]. You been listening at the door again!

BLACKIE. You was speaking loudly.

QUEENY. Your mind is like your body. [*He starts whimpering like a dog.*] Shut up. Anyway if he said it or I said it makes no difference. It does sort of fit in with everything.

BLACKIE. I'll bring you a better one tonight. I got a job at Houghton. I'll bring you the best cloths they got in the house.

QUEENY. All you'll ever bring me is trouble. They'll catch you one day.

BLACKIE. I'll bring you something nice.

QUEENY. If I want anything I can buy it. There are people that do that, you know; who earn what they get and buy what they want. Not like me and you...or Sam over there. This fellow [*points to the table cloth*]...he's living honest.

BLACKIE [*gloomily*]. He'll die poor.

QUEENY. You think that worries him?

BLACKIE. Why do you like him?

QUEENY [*sharply*]. Who said anything about liking? A man comes in

63

here selling table cloths and I buy one. Is that so strange? [*Blacki*
looks at her.] Anyway he's not like everything else. He made me
laugh. Have you ever made me laugh?

BLACKIE. I'll bring you something good tonight.

QUEENY [*ignoring him*]. I liked talking to him. [*She is holding the
cloth, thinking, prepared to put it onto the table.*]

BLACKIE. He said he's not coming back.

[*Queeny stops arranging the cloth. The truth of the words hits her,
she pulls the cloth off and throws it into a corner. She goes back to
the divan, takes another cigarette.*]

BLACKIE. I seen the house we doing tonight. The girl there is
friend. She let me in the other day. They got lots of things; a big
clock like the church that sings the time. You want that? Or
pictures... just so big... I'll bring it to you. Just tell me what
you want.

QUEENY [*with pity*]. It's not your fault, is it, Blackie?

BLACKIE. What do you mean?

QUEENY. That you're the way you are.

BLACKIE. I'm strong, in my arms.

QUEENY [*ignoring what he has said*]. And the same for me. I don't
suppose it's my fault, or even Sam's. [*Pause.*] Then who... who
the hell do you swear at and hate?

[*There is a knock at the door.*]

QUEENY. Who's there?

SAM [*from outside*]. Me.

QUEENY. It's open.

[*Sam comes in. He is about the same age as Queeny, but meticulously
dressed where she is inclined to be slovenly. He is a large and self-
assured man full of the sort of confidence that a little money breeds.
We see him mopping his face with a white handkerchief. In his
movements about the room he frequently stops in front of the mirror
for inspection and small adjustments to his clothing.*]

SAM. They'll be thirsty tomorrow.

QUEENY. They're always thirsty.

SAM. *Ja*, but this weather and pay day will make a difference. You
got enough?

QUEENY. No such thing as enough in the townships. If there was I'd
be out of business.

AM. But I mean for tomorrow. [*Queeny lifts her shoulders in an indifferent gesture.*] I got a case out in the car.

QUEENY. What's it?

AM. Half and half... gin and brandy.

QUEENY. What's your profit, Sam?

AM. Come on, I give it to you cheap. If it was somebody else they'd pay all right, but with you it's different.

QUEENY [*laughs bitterly*]. I been with you too long, Sam, to believe that. Still it's nice to hear you say it.

AM. I like doing business with you, Queeny.

QUEENY. I don't like bargaining.

AM. That's because you know you always get your bargain from me.

QUEENY. Okay, bring it in.

AM [*turning to Blackie who has been sitting in a corner*]. Hey! Get it out of the car.

QUEENY [*coming to Blackie's defence*]. His name is Blackie, just like yours is Sam and mine is Queeny.

AM. Get it out of the car, Blackie...please! [*The last word for Queeny's benefit. Blackie goes out.*] Satisfied?

QUEENY. Ask him. You were speaking to him.

AM. How long are you going to keep him hanging around?

QUEENY. Why shouldn't I?

AM. Why? Because he's going to get us into trouble one day, that's why. Every time I see him he's fighting. He'll kill somebody one day.

QUEENY. He won't if they leave him alone.

AM. Leave him alone!... And him looking like God had the shakes when he made it.

QUEENY. Okay! Let's just say I need him.

AM. You *need* him? That's a new one.

QUEENY. Sure... need him.

AM. What for?

QUEENY. Protection.

AM. And what about me?

QUEENY. What about you?

AM. Don't I protect you?

QUEENY. Do you?

65

SAM. All those years when we was together. Did any man ever get rough with you or beat you up?

QUEENY. No, they never did that.

SAM. So?

QUEENY. So those years are past and better forgotten, and Blackie stays around because it's nice to have a man around.

SAM [*bursting into laughter*]. A man!

QUEENY [*quietly*]. He'll hear you one day, Sam.

SAM. You think I'm frightened.

[*Blackie comes in with the case of liquor from the car. He puts it down and Sam takes over packing away the bottles.*]

BLACKIE [*shuffling up to Queeny*]. I'm going.

QUEENY. Okay.

BLACKIE. It's a good job.

QUEENY. You said that already.

BLACKIE. Don't you want the clock?

QUEENY. If I did I would buy one.

BLACKIE. But I can get this for nothing.

QUEENY. You don't get anything for nothing in this world ... even if you steal it you don't get it for nothing.

BLACKIE. They won't catch me.

QUEENY [*contemptuously*]. They? Who are they? Anyway if they do catch you tell them to go to hell with my regards.

[*Blackie does not understand. He waits uncertainly for Queeny to say something else ... something he will understand. When she doesn't he leaves. Sam has finished packing away the liquor. He pours a drink and then joins Queeny.*]

SAM. Did I say enough? You know you got enough there to start an off-sales. Don't you keep no record of the stuff you get in and what you sell? [*Queeny doesn't think the question worth replying to.*] You know, Queeny, it's all wrong. It goes right against my sense ...

QUEENY. ... of good business.

SAM. *Ja*, that's it. Like I told you ...

QUEENY. You told me once too often, Sam.

SAM. But that's because you won't listen. Now take me and my shop. It's all down in the books. If I want to know how much I'm making I take up the books and there it is ... in black and white.

66

[*Sam has got quite excited about the subject of good business. Queeny is looking at him directly.*]

QUEENY. You like your shop, Sam.

SAM. I waited for it a long time, Queeny. You know that. Like you waited for this.

QUEENY. *Ja*, but it's different. You and your shop and me and this.

SAM. Nonsense. In the old days when we were . . . you know what I mean . . . I used to talk about the shop and you used to talk about having your own shebeen. It was just the same. And we both got what we wanted. I bet if you kept books you'd find you was making more than me.

QUEENY. That only means I'm making good money. It doesn't make anything else the same.

SAM. What else is important?

QUEENY. You haven't changed, Sam.

SAM. If you mean I still believe in this . . . [*rubbing his thumb and forefinger together to indicate money*] you're right. That's the only difference between the full belly I got now and an empty one, between these clothes and rags. And look at you. You got this. What did you have in the old days? This is what we worked for and this is what we got. So let's be happy.

QUEENY. Is it as easy as that?

SAM. What more do you want? Show me another woman around here with half of what you got.

QUEENY. What about the things they got that I haven't?

SAM. Such as?

QUEENY. A man.

SAM [*bursts into rude laughter*]. Didn't you have enough . . . ? [*A deadly look from Queeny kills the laugh.*] Well you know what I mean. What's the matter with you? A man. You'll be saying a home next, with kids . . . and then you've had it. We got no complaints, Queeny. We live comfortable . . . no attachments . . . We're free . . .

QUEENY. Free!

SAM. Yes, free. Who is telling you what to do or where to go? Nobody.

QUEENY. I might even like that for a change.

SAM. A change?

QUEENY. Yes . . . a change from this. You think this is so very different

from the old days? Well let me tell you it's not. You just seen
the outside. You don't know what it's really like. I still sit around
waiting for the night; I still spend the whole day painting my
nails, only now it's not so nice any more 'cause my hands are
getting fat . . . Fat and a little more money. But what else? Nothing.
Just wait for the night and the usual crowd so I can take their
money off them and get a little more rich and a little more fat.
You never thought of it like that, have you, Sam? But you wouldn't
know. Even in the old days you didn't know.

SAM. I looked after the money. If it hadn't been for me where would
you have been?

QUEENY. In the gutter most likely . . . but you cares? *Ja*, that's something else . . . who cares? Who cares a damn?

SAM. I would.

QUEENY. Sure! You'd shake your head for five minutes and then put
somebody else in here 'cause you like your drinks nice and handy.

SAM. You believe that?

QUEENY. Am I wrong?

SAM. After all we been through together?

QUEENY. *You* been through? You don't know half of it. You still
don't and you're not getting any wiser.
[*Now at the window.*] When I stand here during the day I can see
you in the shop, talking like hell to somebody, getting all excited
'cause there's a chance of selling something. And inside here it's
quiet and empty and everything is waiting for the night. When I
look at you I think: He's forgotten. Maybe there wasn't so much
for *him* to forget. I almost hate you when I think that, Sam,
almost hate you.

SAM. You got the blues bad, Queeny.

QUEENY. Blues? You think I'm going to wake up when tomorrow
comes and think life's any better? Anyway, what's it like out
there, are they still asking questions?

SAM. You know people: What's her real name? Where does she
come from? But they're not getting any wiser.

[*Their conversation is interrupted by a knock on the door. Sam opens
it and lets in* Patrick. *The newcomer is about the same age as Sam
but has a false friendly manner and is over-eager to please: the true
'little man'. He is shabbily dressed.*]

PATRICK. Hello, Sam . . . Queeny.

SAM. How's the wife?

PATRICK. [*The expansive smile fades.*] Okay . . . okay . . . It's started.

QUEENY [*making no attempt to conceal her dislike of the man*]. Shouldn't you be with her?

SAM. Leave him alone. Don't you know what a man's like when his wife is having a baby?

QUEENY. If he's the man, the answer is going to be drunk.

SAM. It's a big thing for a man. Patrick just wants a tot to steady his nerves.

PATRICK. *Ja*, that's it. A tot to steady my nerves.

QUEENY. What you got to be nervous about?

SAM. It's his baby.

QUEENY. It's her fifth.

PATRICK [*coming forward hopefully*]. I got a bit of work today, Queeny. I can pay. [*He holds out a few coins in his hand.*]

[*Queeny turns away in disgust at the interpretation he has placed on her reluctance to sell. Patrick is left bewildered. Sam is not so slow. He dips into the outstretched hand and pushes Patrick down into a chair.*]

SAM. Sure you got money. The usual?

PATRICK. *Ja.*

[*Sam serves him with a drink and then comes over to Queeny.*]

SAM. What's the matter with you? He paid.

QUEENY. And his wife?

SAM. He said one drink.

QUEENY. One drink!

SAM. It's not your fault if he doesn't know when to stop.

QUEENY. I'm selling it.

SAM. So you don't sell it? He just goes three houses down and gets it there. You at least sell it to him straight from the bottle. You know how she dilutes. [*Pause.*] It's about time you started as well.

QUEENY. What?

SAM. Diluting. Everybody in this line knows it's legitimate business to dilute a little. These new taxes is making it impossible to give your customers a decent drink at a low price. So you don't want to use water . . . methylated spirits! That's got a kick and I can get

you as much as you want through the shop. Even I been forced
to start. That cheap line of coffee ... any case when you're down
to buying that you expect it.

[*A few memories come back to Sam. He smiles and shakes his head.*]
Water in the liquor! Pea-flour in the coffee! Times have changed.

QUEENY. People were doing that long before we started.

SAM. I mean us. Me and you. We sure got innocent. Because we
scorched this town. We made tham feel they was in hell.

QUEENY. I wasn't so far from feeling that myself at times.

SAM. You don't play with fire without picking up a few blisters. You
know I read somewhere that when the world ends it's going to
be with fire. If that's true you must have been the prophet of bad
times.

QUEENY. Why me?

SAM. You made it hot for a lot of men.

QUEENY. I wasn't the only one.

SAM. I never met another woman that made men sweat like you did
Anyway, they can always say they had their taste of hell before
dying.

QUEENY. What about me? Do you think it was my taste of heaven?

SAM. I'm not saying you liked it.

QUEENY. I'm telling you I hated it.

SAM. We went through it together, Queeny. There's no need to tell
me.

QUEENY. I'm not so sure about that any more.

SAM. You're not trying to say I wasn't there with you?

QUEENY. You were there all right. But I haven't learnt how to laugh
it off and call it the good old days, or how to forget it.

PATRICK [*breaking into the conversation*]. Say ... how about another
tot before I go?

[*Sam gets up and fills Patrick's glass. In the ensuing conversation
Queeny goes back to her divan, lights a cigarette, sits down and
broods.*]

SAM. What you going to call the kid, Patrick?

PATRICK. You know I been sitting here thinking about that.

SAM [*taking a tot for himself and sitting down*]. Well let's hear the
ideas. I never had no kids myself but I got good ideas.

PATRICK. Well I given it a lot of thought. I'm pretty fussy about names. Take mine now... you know I'm named after one of the disciples?

SAM. Patrick?

PATRICK. *Ja*, the disciple of Ireland. That's what they told me up at the church 'cause they gave me the name.

SAM. I was wondering how you got such a good name.

PATRICK. Well now you know.

SAM. Hey! I got a good idea. Why not call it Patrick... after yourself?

PATRICK. And suppose it's a girl?

[*Sam laughs back quietly and flatteringly at the other man's wisdom.*]

SAM. You old...

PATRICK. You see you gotta think. Listen, give me another... it helps me think.

SAM [*passing the bottle*]. Of course.

QUEENY [*breaking into the conversation*]. You've had enough.

SAM. Look, the man's thinking! There's going to be something out there just now that's going to want a name and Patrick here is finding it. Aren't you?

PATRICK. Just like that.

SAM. So he can go home and walk right in and say hello... whatever its name is going to be... Isn't that so?

PATRICK. Just so.

SAM [*pouring another tot and taking Patrick's money*]. So we can't call it Patrick.

PATRICK. Nuh. But I think I got one... Augustine.

SAM. What's that?

PATRICK. Another disciple.

SAM. You can't have a whole family of disciples... and suppose it's a girl?

PATRICK. I'm prepared. Augustina!

SAM [*with a wry face and sceptically*]. Augustina? That's a mouthful.

PATRICK [*the look of triumph fading; uncertainly*]. You think so?

SAM. Of course. Go on, try it... go on... Try calling August... whatever it is aloud. Go on.

PATRICK [*opening his mouth, then abandoning the attempt*]. *Ja*, maybe you're right.

SAM. You want something short and snappy... 'cause that's modern.

You take the names of things today, like . . . Let me see . . . Jik.
[*Repeats it.*] . . . Jik.

PATRICK [*incredulous*]. Jik?

SAM. *Ja* . . . that stuff that cleans . . . Or Coke . . . there's another one.
I'm not suggesting you call the kid after a cold drink, but think
along those lines. This Augustina stuff is out.

[*A knock at the door interrupts the discussion between the two men.
Sam gets up and goes to the door, opens it and peers out. A few works
are spoken, including a very loud 'What' from Sam, who turns back
to Queeny.*]

SAM. Will you please come and tell somebody that we don't serve
coffee?

[*Queeny looks up, for a moment not realizing who is outside. When
she does, she stands up, unbelievingly. All trace of boredom has
vanished. Sam goes back to his chair and watches the next few
minutes from that position. Queeny lets Johnny in.*]

JOHNNY. I missed my bus, so I thought I'd take that cup of coffee
after all.

QUEENY. Sure . . . sure . . . sit down. I'll put the kettle on. [*Moves to
the door, pauses.*] How did it go? [*She goes into the kitchen.*]

JOHNNY [*calling after her*]. You was right. I didn't sell any more.

SAM. What?

JOHNNY. Table cloths.

SAM. Table cloths.

JOHNNY. I sell table cloths. [*Seeing the table is uncovered, he looks
for the one he sold Queeny.*] Where's the one I sold her? [*He finds
it in a corner.*]

SAM [*surprise turning into veiled resentment and dislike; it is obvious
that these two are not going to like each other*]. What do you think
you are going to do with that?

JOHNNY [*ignoring the tone*]. Put it on the table. I sold it to her 'cause
this table was getting marks from all the glasses.

SAM [*sarcastic*]. Now isn't that a pity.

JOHNNY. It is. It's a good table.

SAM [*turning back to Patrick, deliberately ignoring Johnny*]. Well, we're
having a private conversation.

JOHNNY [*refusing to be ignored*]. Aren't you used to table cloths or
something?

SAM [*nettled*]. Look, I don't know who you are, where you come
from or what you do . . .

JOHNNY. Name's Johnny, I come from Alex and I sell table cloths.
And you?

SAM. A friend . . . a very good friend.

JOHNNY. In that case I don't see how you can mind me putting this
on the table.

[*There is a dangerous little moment that could easily become nasty
but for Queeny's entrance into the room. Seeing Johnny with the red
table cloth in his hand she comes up apologetically.*]

QUEENY. Oh yes, the table cloth . . . I hadn't put it on 'cause I
wanted to clean the table proper first. But I'll do it now. [*She
takes a rag, forces the men to lift their glasses, wipes the table off
and then puts the cloth down.*]

JOHNNY. Looks good, doesn't it?

SAM. Looks like any other table cloth to me . . . and not such a good
line at that.

JOHNNY. I never said it cost much . . . I don't charge much.

QUEENY. Who says that's important? It matches in with everything
else like you said.

SAM. Sounds like you two had a long talk about table cloths.

[*Queeny doesn't answer, but the look she gives him is warning enough.
He shuts up, pours himself another tot. Patrick also gets a drink.
Queeny turns her attention to Johnny. There is a small embarrassed
pause.*]

QUEENY. Sit down while you're waiting for the coffee. It won't be
long . . . [*Johnny sits.*] Or maybe you're in a hurry to get home.

JOHNNY. Should I be?

QUEENY. Folks waiting for you . . . wife maybe.

JOHNNY. I got nobody.

QUEENY. You look the sort.

JOHNNY. What sort is that?

QUEENY. Wife and kids . . . maybe a home.

JOHNNY. Why do you say that?

QUEENY. You just do. I seen them before . . . people trying to do
something with their lives.

JOHNNY. Aren't you?

QUEENY [*laughing*]. You say the damndest things.

JOHNNY. Well...

QUEENY. Let's say, I'm hanging on to what I got.

JOHNNY. Maybe making it a bit bigger as well.

QUEENY [*laughing quietly*]. *Ja*. That's not much, is it?

JOHNNY. Depends. I knew a fellow once... had a horse and an ol
cart... people used to laugh at him 'cause he didn't make mucl
and what he had he always spent on the horse and the cart
Sometimes he went without supper just so the horse could eat
Everyone thought he was mad but he carried on like they wasn'
there. One day I asked him: Joe, why don't you sell that horse
and buy yourself some good clothes and eat well for a month. H
looked at me: What do I do after the month? Get a job, I said
like everybody else. He shook his head: Johnny, you're asking m
to sell my freedom for a good meal and clothes. I thought a lo
about what he said. That horse meant nobody could call him 'boy'
or say do this or that. He was his own boss. Maybe it's like tha
with you.

QUEENY [*thoughtfully*]. I got a little money. That's all I'm hangin
on to.

JOHNNY. That's a big word.

QUEENY. What?

JOHNNY. Money. It could mean security, three meals a day, a roo
over your head and independence... like Joe.

QUEENY. And you?

JOHNNY. Me?

QUEENY. *Ja*, you. What you doing?

JOHNNY. Same as Joe.

QUEENY. Horse and cart.

JOHNNY. No, my own boss.

QUEENY. How long you been like that?

JOHNNY. Off and on. I'd hoped these table cloths would be my rea
break. If I'd made some money I was going to try something good

QUEENY. What was that?

JOHNNY. What's the use. [*Gesturing towards the suitcase.*] The
haven't sold. I'll be looking for a job on Monday.

QUEENY. You're not going to like that.

JOHNNY. Would you? Get a couple of quid a month so somebod

can kick you around and feel like a white man. Old Joe was right.

SAM. [*He has been listening to the conversation, now breaks in.*] What's old Joe going to do when the horse dies? Make biltong. [*Laughter.*]

QUEENY [*annoyed*]. Can't you keep your mouth shut, Sam?

SAM. I'm just interested in old Joe. No harm in asking.

JOHNNY. Joe died before the horse.

SAM. Too bad, too bad . . . Would have been nice to know what he would have done. It's also bad about old Joe dying, of course. But that's not exactly progress, is it? Dying with only a horse and cart, and maybe just dying before the horse 'cause that was also getting old.

QUEENY. What you trying to do, Sam?

SAM. Just joining in a conversation, Queeny. Of course if it was private . . .

QUEENY. Maybe it is.

SAM. Okay. I'll be back when it's not so crowded. [*Sam goes out.*]

QUEENY. Don't pay no attention to him.

JOHNNY. Me pay attention to him? It was the other way around. Is he your partner?

QUEENY. Just a friend. He's got the shop across the street. Comes in here for his drinks.

JOHNNY. And that chap I saw this afternoon? The hunchback.

QUEENY. You mean Blackie.

JOHNNY. That's the name.

QUEENY. Also a friend. [*Johnny just nods his head.*] You're thinking I got strange friends.

JOHNNY. Maybe. I don't know much about shebeens.

QUEENY. Blackie's not the same as Sam. He's ugly, all right . . . but then he was born that way. He didn't choose it. If he was straight I think he would have been a good man. But being crooked like that nobody has given him a chance.

JOHNNY. He's got a good friend.

QUEENY. Me? I don't know. A lot of kids was teasing him one day, I watched it through the window. What got me was the big people standing around doing nothing . . . Some of them was smiling, they thought it funny. I went out and swore the whole lot of them into hell. I just wanted them to stop, that's all. But Blackie

hung around. For two days he just sat outside there on the pavement watching me come and go. Every time I looked out of the
window he was sitting there. So I called him in and gave him
some food ... he's been hanging around ever since.

I'll get that coffee.

[*Queeny goes into her kitchen. Patrick, disturbed by the sudden
silence, looks up from his glass and sees Johnny. Patrick is drunk.*]

PATRICK. Edward.

JOHNNY. What?

PATRICK. And if it's a girl ... Edwina.

JOHNNY. Who's that?

PATRICK. My kid.

JOHNNY. You got a kid.

PATRICK [*an edge of despair and cynicism to his words*]. Have I got a
kid! [*Lifting his glass.*] This is my fifth ... Kid, I mean. This is
my fifth kid and it should be here by now. I been sitting here
trying to find a decent name for it 'cause that's all I'm ever likely
to give it. That's not much, huh?

JOHNNY. Why don't you go back to your wife?

PATRICK. You think I'm drunk. Maybe I am. But I only meant to
have one. You see this is my fifth ... Child, I mean, it's my fifth
child. When you already got four and another comes along ... I
dunno ... it's sort of too much. You sort of sit here and wish it
wasn't coming and that is a hell of a start for it, isn't it? I only
wanted one drink but when I got to thinking like that, I had
another to try and stop myself. And now I'm saying I wish it
wasn't coming. You got kids?

JOHNNY. No.

PATRICK. Don't.

JOHNNY. Why?

PATRICK. It's hell. In every way it's hell. You know they should make
it that we blacks can't have babies ... 'cause hell they made it so
we can't give them no chances when they come. They just about
made it so we can't live. But with babies it's hell! They cry,
you don't get no sleep, they need things ... and they suck the old
woman dry. God, she's a wreck. And she was a woman. I mean
I wouldn't have married her if she wasn't. You see what I mean
don't you?

[*Patrick accidentally spills his drink over Johnny.*] How did that happen?

JOHNNY. It's okay.

PATRICK. Hell . . . I'm sorry . . .

JOHNNY. Forget it.

[*Queeny comes in with coffee.*]

QUEENY. What happened?

JOHNNY. Just an accident.

QUEENY. Him?

JOHNNY. Forget it.

QUEENY [*to Patrick*]. You messy little bastard.

PATRICK. We was just having a chat and I . . .

QUEENY. And as usual you didn't know when to stop.

JOHNNY. Forget it, Queeny. It's an old jacket.

QUEENY. First you mess up your own life and then you want to make a mess of everybody else's.

PATRICK. I paid you.

QUEENY. Get the hell out of here.

PATRICK. Okay.

QUEENY. Get out.

JOHNNY. Easy, Queeny, it was just an accident.

QUEENY. Keep out of this, Johnny.

JOHNNY. I don't see why I must. He spilt it over me.

QUEENY. Are you standing up for him?

JOHNNY. I'm standing up for nobody.

QUEENY. Then keep out of it. [*To Patrick.*] I said get out.

JOHNNY. Have a heart, Queeny.

QUEENY. With trash like him?

JOHNNY. His money was all right wasn't it?

[*Sam comes in.*]

SAM. One of your kids outside, Patrick. Says the baby's arrived. They want you over at your place.

[*Patrick stands up unsteadily. Sam, having poured himself a drink, turns his attention to Patrick.*]

SAM. What you going to call it?

[*Patrick has a glass in one hand, the other in his pocket. He takes out the latter and looks at it. It holds the last of the money he brought in with him . . . a sixpence.*]

PATRICK. Sixpence.

SAM. Sixpence! Hey, that's good.

[*Patrick lifts his glass to his lips. He doesn't drink. Sam's laugh releases his pent-up bitterness. He smashes the glass to the floor and moves to the door.*]

QUEENY. Wait!

[*Patrick stops, turns. Queeny is sorting out the money on the table.*] Here is every penny you spent here tonight. [*She throws a handful of coins at Patrick's feet. He bends down and picks them up.*] Take it and get out . . . and don't come back.

[*Patrick exits.*]

SAM [*who has watched Queeny's last actions with disbelief*]. What's this? Hand-out time at the mission?

[*Queeny doesn't answer.*]

You going mad or something? He didn't give you back the drinks he bought.

QUEENY [*to Johnny*]. You satisfied?

JOHNNY. Why ask me?

QUEENY. You made me do it.

JOHNNY. I didn't say anything.

QUEENY. Okay, you didn't say anything, but you made me do it. I could see it written all over your face, the 'good' looking at the 'bad'. I lived with that look too long not to know it.

JOHNNY. Shall I go?

QUEENY. No! Please . . . I don't know what's got into me.

SAM. And neither do I. If that's how you're going to carry on we might as well . . .

QUEENY. It was my money, Sam, and this is my place. It's got nothing to do with you.

[*These words stop Sam. It is the first time Queeny has ever thrown his words back in his face. He drops back to a chair against the wall and watches the developments.*]

QUEENY [*to Johnny*]. I been getting sick of it lately. It's not much of life is it?

JOHNNY. You know.

QUEENY. [*She fetches a broom and sweeps up the pieces of broken glass.*] Well, it's not. I'm telling you it's not. It doesn't mean anything

78

when you get your money from bums like him...Not if that's the only way you've ever got money...selling something that he's ashamed of or...you're ashamed of. I know what he felt like when he smashed that glass. 'If only it was my life lying in pieces on the floor.' Just sweep them away and start all over again. But you're stuck with it...him, me...Blackie...There's somebody else who wouldn't mind taking it apart and putting it together again, with a few improvements. But where do you start? You think I'm mad?

JOHNNY. Just never heard a woman talk like that before.

QUEENY. And it sounds crazy.

JOHNNY. It sounds like sense.

QUEENY. *Ja*?

JOHNNY. I know what you mean. I also felt like that.

QUEENY. You?

JOHNNY. I'm no different.

QUEENY. You're not like Patrick.

JOHNNY. I'm younger, that's all. When he was my age...

QUEENY. No, Johnny, when you're his age you'll be different. It's like I said, you're trying to do something with your life. Me? I'm in business because I got some money and there's plenty of bums like Patrick. But what else could I do?

JOHNNY. Sell table cloths.

QUEENY. You're laughing at yourself.

JOHNNY. It's a joke, isn't it. I'm the man who's doing something with his life and the first thing I try...nothing doing. My own boss but I'll be looking for a job on Monday.

QUEENY. No use talking like that. So the first thing you tried didn't work. You just got to try something else.

JOHNNY. Such as?

QUEENY. Medicines! There's something everybody buys. Try selling that.

JOHNNY. It wouldn't be the same. It's not just a question of selling something. I...never mind.

QUEENY. Go on.

JOHNNY. It's another funny story.

QUEENY. I didn't laugh at the last one.

JOHNNY. Well you see, I just don't want to sell. I'm not a salesman. In fact it's hard for me to sell...you saw that yourself this morning. I want to start my own business.

QUEENY. Doing what?

JOHNNY. I worked with a white chap who was an interior decorator. You know what that is? [*Queeny shakes her head.*] It's got to do with the way you fix up your house. The interior decorator gives you ideas about what you must buy, and how you must match things. Like this table cloth...Remember me saying the red one? ...that it's your colour...well that's interior decorating on a sort of small scale. I mean I would only operate on a small scale 'cause our people just don't have the money to do it in a big way. I was actually going to concentrate on one line, materials...You know, curtains, bedspreads, cushion covers...that sort of thing.

QUEENY. Sounds like you'd need a bit of money to get started.

JOHNNY. No. I thought of a great idea. The big factories that make materials sell a lot of bits and pieces cheap...sometimes there's something small wrong with it or maybe it's just a piece left over. But they let it go cheap. I was going to buy a lot of that and sell it with my ideas. You see I got a feeling for matching things... the white chap told me. I'd come to a house and give the woman ideas. Like...take this room. You see that window. Yellow curtains! What that window needs is yellow curtains. This is a dark room and that colour would liven things up. It would go with your table cloth. And next month when I come around again you take something with yellow and red for your bed...and cushions with red in them. Can you see the difference?

QUEENY [*genuinely pleased*]. You got good ideas, Johnny.

JOHNNY. You see, it's important, Queeny...trying to make life better. I'm not saying my idea is going to change the world, but maybe it will give us a bit more guts, and make waking up tomorrow a little bit easier. You said you were getting sick of life the way it is...so why don't you start changing things? You could start with this room.

QUEENY. What's wrong with it?

JOHNNY. Nothing...if you got no complaints. But you sounded like you had plenty. So you put up those yellow curtains...a vase with some flowers on this table...a little mat at the door so that nobody starts tramping mud into the room.

QUEENY. I think I'd like that.

JOHNNY. Of course you would. And you'd start getting proud ... and *then* let anybody try leaving marks on your table, or on your cloth, or messing up your floor.

QUEENY. I'm your first customer, Johnny. When do you start?

JOHNNY. When? Looks like never. The table cloths. Remember the table cloths? I sold one today ... to you. They were supposed to be my start. If I'd sold them I would have had ten quid ...

QUEENY. Ten pounds? Is that enough?

JOHNNY. I tell you I checked. I went down to the factory and saw what I could have bought with ten quid. There was more than I could have carried away. But they haven't sold.

QUEENY. You're not going to let that stop you.

JOHNNY. They didn't sell. There's nothing I can do about that.

QUEENY. Get your money somewhere else.

JOHNNY. Where?

QUEENY [*after a pause*]. Me.

JOHNNY. You?

QUEENY. Why not?

JOHNNY. Why? ... Why? Because it's just silly, that's why.

QUEENY. Why is it silly?

JOHNNY. Look, don't you be silly as well.

QUEENY. Well, tell me why you can't borrow ten quid from me.

JOHNNY. Because it's ten quid.

QUEENY. I take that much in here on a bad night.

JOHNNY. Because you never saw me before today.

QUEENY. I trust you.

JOHNNY. Because you don't know if the idea is worth anything at all.

QUEENY. We'll never answer that one without first trying.

JOHNNY. Look, Queeny, just drop it. I didn't come in here for that.

QUEENY. I'm not saying you did. You didn't ask me. I offered.

JOHNNY. No.

QUEENY. Johnny ... suppose I want to. Suppose I really want to.

JOHNNY. But why? You're making better money here than I will ever get from selling rags.

QUEENY. You saw how. Did you like what you saw? Answer me.

JOHNNY. [*Pause.*] No.

QUEENY. And you talked a lot about changing things. Give me a chance.

JOHNNY. But if it doesn't work . . . I can't pay you back.

QUEENY. Ten pounds isn't going to break me, Johnny. In any case I want to be your partner . . . I want to be part of it. You got the idea, I give the money. That's fair isn't it?

[*Johnny is beginning to waver.*]

JOHNNY. It might work.

QUEENY. Of course it would. When I heard your ideas I thought they was good. I would have bought. Other women will be the same.

JOHNNY. I've worked it out at fifty per cent profit.

QUEENY. That's good legitimate business.

JOHNNY. And there's big possibilities . . . I mean for expansion.

QUEENY. *Ja?*

JOHNNY. Sure. To begin with, I'd sell the material myself, going from door to door. But if it catches on and the profit is like I said . . . well, we'd build up a big stock and that could mean a shop.

QUEENY. With them coming to us.

JOHNNY. You've got the idea.

QUEENY. A shop . . . with counters, and all the stuff behind . . . And a name! We got to have a name for the shop.

JOHNNY. We'd find one.

[*At this point the door opens quietly and Blackie comes in. He is holding a clock. During the ensuing scene he tries with small furtive gestures to catch Queeny's attention. It is obviously her clock, but in the excitement of her talk with Johnny she does not see him.*]

QUEENY. We'd open it up at nine in the morning. That's the time any decent shop opens, and we'd be busy with all the customers coming and going and at five o'clock we'd close up, count up our money and think about tomorrow. You know something?

JOHNNY. What?

QUEENY. We'd be respectable.

JOHNNY. There's nothing to be ashamed of.

QUEENY. Johnny, it's the best thing I've ever heard of. When do we start?

JOHNNY. Well . . . look Queeny, don't you want to think about it for a day or so . . .

[*Her answer is to go to the sideboard, take out her money box, count*] *out ten notes and put them on the table in front of Johnny.*]

QUEENY. There. I thought about it and that's my answer.

JOHNNY. Right now?

QUEENY. Take advice from somebody who knows ... don't waste time or chances. Now. Tomorrow's pay day around here. Get your material in the morning and sell in the afternoon. That's when the women get back with their men's pay. [*Johnny still hesitates.*] Take it! If we don't start now maybe we will never.

JOHNNY. I can be down at the factory first thing and then come here when I got the material.

QUEENY. I'll be waiting.

JOHNNY. I can't believe it.

QUEENY. Do you think I can? Nothing like this has happened to me before.

JOHNNY. I'm going. [*Takes his suitcase.*] I'll leave these cloths and try and sell them as well, but the suitcase I need for the material.

QUEENY. Buy big, Johnny.

JOHNNY. You leave that to me [*He is at the door.*] Thanks, Queeny.

QUEENY. Till tomorrow.

[*Johnny exits. She watches the door close behind him, her face shining and happy.*]

QUEENY. Sam ...

SAM. You gone mad or something?

QUEENY [*ignoring the remark*]. Sam, you got yellow material?

SAM. Look, I don't know what was in that coffee, but sober up, will you! You just let ten quid walk out of your life without even a farewell tear.

QUEENY. It will be back. Now how about that yellow material?

SAM. Look, Queeny, I'm being serious. That was ten quid we worked for.

QUEENY. I worked for.

SAM. Okay! So I just don't like seeing a friend lose it. You think you going to see it or that rag-bag man again?

QUEENY. Tomorrow.

SAM. Queeny! I've also tried that racket.

QUEENY. That was you. This is Johnny.

SAM. Will you wake up!!

QUEENY. I have! And for the first time in my life. I've woken up to something that looks like it might be fun and nice and clean. And don't shout at me Sam. Material ... yellow material. You got some?

SAM. Okay, if you don't mind making a fool of yourself and losing ten quid ...

QUEENY. Yellow material!!!

SAM [*irritably*]. Sure I got yellow material. I got everything.

QUEENY. I want some. Enough for curtains.

SAM. I'll send it over in the morning.

QUEENY. I want it now.

SAM. Now ... ?

QUEENY. Yes, now! Fetch it. I'll use as much as I want and give you back the rest. Well, what are you waiting for?

[*Sam leaves. Queeny has in the meantime managed to get down the curtains. Blackie, alone with her at last, comes forward. She bumps into him.*]

QUEENY. Blackie! What have you got there?

[*Blackie says nothing, just holds up the clock.*]

I told you I didn't want it. Go give it to Sam to sell.

[*Blackie is still holding the clock outstretched as Queeny returns to her work at the curtains. She is humming softly. The clock in Blackie's hand begins to chime.*]

CURTAIN

ACT TWO

Scene 1

Queeny's shebeen the next morning. It is empty. The room has changed ... yellow curtains, table cloth, and a vase of flowers. After a few seconds Blackie, *still carrying his clock, comes in through the street door.*

QUEENY [*from the kitchen*]. That you, Johnny?

[*Queeny enters from the other room. Her excitement dies when she sees that it is only Blackie.*]

BLACKIE. Nobody else got one what sings like the church. Listen! [*He moves the hands of the clock and it begins to chime.*]

QUEENY. Which way did you come?

BLACKIE. Along the street.

QUEENY. Did you see the chap who was here last night?

BLACKIE. Him.

QUEENY. Yes, him. Did you see him?

BLACKIE. No. Sam said he wasn't going to come.

QUEENY. Sam says everything.

BLACKIE. Sam says . . .

QUEENY. I'm sick of hearing what Sam says. What's the time? [*Blackie lifts up the clock for her to see.*] That thing's crazy. Why do you carry it around if it don't tell the time?

BLACKIE. But you don't listen. [*He moves the hands again.*]

QUEENY [*impatiently*]. I've heard it once and it doesn't change it's tune.

BLACKIE. Why you shouting at me? I done nothing.

QUEENY [*collecting herself*]. I'm jumpy this morning.

BLACKIE. You remember what I said! I do anything for you if you don't shout or laugh at me.

QUEENY. Okay, Blackie! [*Pause during which she looks around the room desperately.*] Let's do something. These curtains . . . *ja* . . . maybe there's still time for that. Give me a hand.
[*With Blackie's assistance she gets down the old curtain around the divan. She proceeds to sew on extra rings.*]

QUEENY. Why you staring at me like that?

BLACKIE. You doing that for him.

QUEENY. What's so strange about sewing a few rings onto a curtain?

BLACKIE. You never down it before.

QUEENY. So I'm doing it now.

BLACKIE. You never done no sewing or fixing up like this before.

QUEENY. You said that already. Don't always repeat yourself. It's a bad habit you got. My hearing's all right.

BLACKIE. This chap . . . is he going to make you like other women?

QUEENY. What do you mean? I am a woman.

[*Sam enters from the street.*]

QUEENY. What's the time, Sam?

SAM [*chuckling*]. So you're getting worried.

QUEENY. The time, Sam.

SAM [*speaking very deliberately*]. He's half an hour late already.. according to my reckoning. And I've been generous. I had him out of bed at eight . . . which you must admit is not too early for a man starting off on a new business venture . . . I gave him half an hour from Alex to town . . . might have missed the first bus . . half an hour choosing his goods and half an hour coming out here and another half just in case he stopped over somewhere. That makes ten . . . which it was half an hour ago. Of course there could, as they say, be a weak link in the chain. And according to my acquaintance with human nature the weak link in this case is the first one. That getting out of bed at eight to swap a crisp ten quid for a heap of rags? If you do you're not the same woman the cleaned up this town with me. Ten quid on rags! Like I told you it's an old racket.

   More likely than not he's lying nice and comfortable in bed right now thinking about spending that money. Don't forget it's not every day that you can pick up ten quid like that. [*Clicking his fingers.*] However, old Sam never deserts a friend. When you get around to waking up, send this yellow stuff back and I'll sell it for you . . . make it a fancy line and double the price. That way we should get your loss down to about nine quid.

QUEENY. If you so much as touch those curtains you'll never come in here again.

SAM. I was only trying to do you a favour. Of course they don't look too bad now you come to think of it. Maybe he did have a few good ideas after all. Pity he wasn't straight.

QUEENY. What I said about touching those curtains goes for your mouth as well . . . Say something else like that . . .

SAM. When are you going to wake up, Queeny?

QUEENY. I woke up last night, Sam, and don't ask too many questions otherwise I'm going to tell you what some things look like now that I got my eyes open.

SAM. Okay, I'll shut up. [*Picks a flower for his buttonhole.*] Anyway what is ten quid on pay day! Maybe I'm being a little tight.

QUEENY. With my money.

SAM. You're my friend. I just don't want you to turn around and say I let you down. I never done it in the old days.

QUEENY. The only reason you never let me down is because we were already at the bottom. Anyway I don't want no more talk about the old days ... not to me or anybody else.

SAM. I get you [*turning to go*]. [*He pauses at the door*.] But don't forget them.

QUEENY. Why?

SAM. So you don't expect what you didn't buy. None of our customers thought they was getting a wife for our price. You paid ten quid last night for a small kick and nothing else.

BLACKIE [*shuffling forward to Queeny; it is obvious that she is upset*]. You want me to go to Alex and get your money? I'll find him and bring it back. Okay?

QUEENY. Get out.

BLACKIE. Tonight I'll ...

QUEENY. Just leave me alone.

[*Blackie takes up his clock and goes. A few seconds later the door which was left slightly ajar swings open and Johnny comes in carrying his suitcase*.]

QUEENY [*not looking around*]. I told you to get out!

JOHNNY. It wasn't me you told.

QUEENY. Johnny!

JOHNNY. That's your man, plus the finest selection of material any township has ever seen.

QUEENY. Johnny!

JOHNNY. You been crying or something?

QUEENY. I thought you wasn't coming.

JOHNNY. And you cried? Well you can stop 'cause I'm here and just take a look at this.

[*He opens his suitcase. A flood of coloured material spills out onto the floor. For Queeny it is a moment of release which starts with a gasp of surprise*.]

And you wanted to know if ten pounds was enough? Well there's all this and I still got two quid in my pocket. But take a good look at the colours. Red ...

QUEENY. Blue ... green ...

JOHNNY. Yellow... purple...

QUEENY. You brought in the rainbow, man.

JOHNNY. And the sizes... see this one.

QUEENY [*taking a large length of red from his hands and draping* ‹
round her]. My colour, Johnny.

JOHNNY. That's a curtain you're wearing... and what about this fo‹
a bed? And cushions to match!

QUEENY. I never seen so much colour.

JOHNNY. How does it make you feel?

QUEENY. Excited.

JOHNNY. Well, don't be scared. Come on, touch it... get the fee‹
of it, you'll be handling a lot.

QUEENY. You really think so, Johnny?

JOHNNY. Now that I actually see it I say we can't go wrong. You‹
know when I was walking up the street with this material th‹
women came out of their houses to see what I had. They wante‹
to buy it there and then. I got two names already. I got to be ther‹
this afternoon when they get back with their men's pay... an‹
let me tell you they are going to buy. I got scared last night whe‹
you offered me the money so suddenly. But now! This is wha‹
I've been waiting for, Queeny. I got so many ideas up here m‹
head is bursting. Number one. The place that sold me this als‹
sells feathers and fluff for cushions, you buy it by the box. So w‹
are going to make the cushions complete ourselves. You got
sewing machine?

QUEENY. No. But I can buy one.

JOHNNY. No. You've given your share. The machine comes out o‹
the profits... maybe in a month or so. Then you can do som‹
stitching while I'm out selling.

QUEENY. I don't know how to sew.

JOHNNY. So you learn. Other women can, you can. You're the sam‹
as them.

QUEENY. Say that again.

JOHNNY. I said you're like the other women. Anything wrong?

QUEENY. Nothing. Nothing at all. I just wanted to hear you say it.

JOHNNY. Now to work.

QUEENY. But you just come in. Aren't you tired? Carrying all that?

JOHNNY. Tired today?

QUEENY. But breakfast. I got something cooking.

JOHNNY. Okay. Bring it in.

[*Queeny goes to the kitchen to fetch his breakfast. Johnny starts sorting out his material.*]

QUEENY[*from the other room*]. When you going to start?

JOHNNY. Straight after I've eaten. This is make–or–break day for me, and I want to know which it is.

QUEENY [*in the doorway*]. Nothing could break today, Johnny. Even if you came home with nothing sold.

JOHNNY. Hey, don't say that!

QUEENY. It's just that I'm so happy.

JOHNNY. We might have something to celebrate tonight.

QUEENY. I got to think about that.

JOHNNY. What?

QUEENY. Our celebration.

JOHNNY. Here?

QUEENY. Of course.

JOHNNY. But isn't this your big night? Pay day?

QUEENY. What do you mean?

JOHNNY. The shebeen.

QUEENY. I'd forgotten.

JOHNNY. There's big money in it. You said so yourself last night.

QUEENY. Big money. [*With bitterness.*] Did you have to remind me?

JOHNNY. We can celebrate tomorrow.

QUEENY. No. This is our day, and I'm not going to let a lot of bums bugger it up. You saw what it was like last night. Tonight's going to be worse. The whole place full of them!...moaning and slobbering until it drives you mad.

JOHNNY. Take it easy.

QUEENY. Take it easy! I've taken it far too long and it hasn't been easy. And I'm not taking it tonight. Johnny, the shebeen can go to hell tonight.

JOHNNY. These fellows are your customers. That's not good business.

QUEENY. Don't talk like Sam.

JOHNNY. Sam's got a point there if you want to keep the shebeen.

QUEENY. And what if I don't?

[*Johnny is stuck for words. Queeny comes up to him. She picks up a*

89

piece of material to emphasize her next point.]
We've started this haven't we? Maybe...

JOHNNY. Maybe it doesn't work.

QUEENY. It will.

JOHNNY. But suppose...

QUEENY. It's going to, Johnny.

JOHNNY. Please! I'm asking you to give me a chance. I'll go out there just now and do my damnedest to sell... but don't make me scared to come back. Let's just see how it goes.

QUEENY. But this is our day, Johnny. Look, just for tonight. I'll tell them the police raided me. If I got to start selling again tomorrow, okay. But I can't tonight. Please, Johnny.

JOHNNY. It's your business, Queeny.

QUEENY. You can sell those and leave the rest to me.
[*Johnny cannot argue. She goes back to the kitchen, re-enters with food, and lays it out on the table.*]

QUEENY. Okay.

JOHNNY. You know, I am hungry. When you're excited like this you don't get time to think about food.

QUEENY. That's my job.

JOHNNY. Cooking for me?

QUEENY. I like it. You know I never cooked for any man before.

JOHNNY. Nobody has done any cooking for me.

QUEENY. No one?

JOHNNY. That's what I said.

QUEENY. Your girl friend.

JOHNNY. Never had one.

QUEENY. You're joking.

JOHNNY. I'm not.

QUEENY. Why?

JOHNNY. I've never looked for one.

QUEENY. When you get around to it, what are you going to look for?

JOHNNY. Lots of things.

QUEENY. Tell me.

JOHNNY. She's going to be clean.

QUEENY [*laughing*]. Clean.

JOHNNY. Live and think clean! You can always wash your hands, or your face or your feet. But your mind? Could you wash that if you got to thinking dirt or living like it? I touched real filth once...never again!

QUEENY. You had it tough Johnny?

JOHNNY. No more nor less than anybody else with a black skin. The trouble is a little means so damned much if you think and feel a lot. But there I go talking about my troubles. Tell me about yourself, Queeny. You know I don't even know your real name.

QUEENY. Rose.

JOHNNY. Why do you run away from it?

QUEENY. Who said anything about running away?

JOHNNY. Well, why did you drop it?

QUEENY. People started calling me Queeny. It stuck.

JOHNNY. I'm going to call you Rose.

QUEENY. Don't.

JOHNNY. It's as good as Queeny.

QUEENY. Please, Johnny, don't.

JOHNNY. Okay.

QUEENY. Just let's say I like Queeny better.

JOHNNY. You been here long?

QUEENY. Four or five years. Does that sound long. Maybe it is. But there's been nothing in it...nothing I couldn't tell you in one minute. I got fatter, certainly richer, but there's nothing else. You know what's the secret of keeping alive?

JOHNNY. You tell me.

QUEENY. It's to keep wanting things.

JOHNNY. Then I got a long life ahead of me.

QUEENY. That's what I mean. You'll always be doing things, thinking up new ideas, and that's going to keep you going. Me? I just rolled over and died.

JOHNNY. Isn't there anything you want, Queeny?

QUEENY. There is now. But there was a time I thought I had all I wanted when I got this. But when I had it, that was the end. There's been times I never knew what day it was in here...and I never needed to know. I'd wake up and think is it Monday or Tuesday, maybe Friday? It didn't make any difference. Giving it a name didn't make it any different from the rest.

I worked too hard and waited too long for this. That is where I
made my mistake. Since I was a kid and my father used to
drink his pay packet down on a Friday night while we waited
hungry at home...since those days I said to myself, 'One day
you'll have a shebeen and get fat.' Strange the things kids think,
huh?

JOHNNY. How many in the family?

QUEENY. Six of us when my mother died. It might have been
different if she'd stayed alive. She was one of those people who..
well, like you say, lived clean. We was so poor we didn't even
have any rubbish, but she swept out that room as if it was filthy.
When she died I got out.

JOHNNY. The others?

QUEENY. I don't know. I still ask myself that one. You see I was the
oldest, the youngest was still drinking from my mother. I should
have stayed and tried to help them...I mean you know what kids
are like, small, helpless, hungry. Now you know something about
me. Not so good, is it?

JOHNNY. You mean running away?

QUEENY. And leaving the others.

JOHNNY. You was a kid.

QUEENY. I try to tell myself that, but it doesn't always work. Like
you said, you can't wash your mind as easily as your hands.
[*Pause.*] But if somebody tried hard enough, could they?...Wash
off something from the past?

JOHNNY. Depends on the person, I guess.

QUEENY. And other people.

JOHNNY. Why them?

QUEENY. If you were trying to forget something, but others kept
reminding you of it...wouldn't work, would it?

JOHNNY. [*Pause.*] You may have had it rough, Queeny, but I had
my face rubbed in dirt. I know what it smells like, what it
tastes like. That's how close I was to it and that's why I hate it.
I was a kid. Seventeen years old. It was the big story about the
mines. The good food, the clean rooms, the money. My parents
bought that one all right. Money! So I came here, ten years ago.
I stood just one year in that place. A fellow can't take more. Did
you hear what I said? I said a fellow can't take more.

QUEENY. Okay, Johnny, I heard you.

JOHNNY. You might have heard me okay, but do you know what I mean? There's no women in those compounds and they don't let you out. There's big bursting men in those compounds and there's no women. So they take the boys, the young ones, like me. That's what they take.

QUEENY. Okay, Johnny.

JOHNNY. Stop saying that because it's not okay. It's like dogs, see.

QUEENY. Johnny!

JOHNNY. Yes, dogs, or something else that crawls around the garbage cans or the gutter. Something dirty! I've tried to wash it off, Queeny. I've tried. Every day, I try. But there is always something around that brings it back. Like that bus ride in from Alex this morning. It was hell. It was crowded with men, big men. I could feel the violence in their bodies. Like the nights in the compound when they sat around and spoke about women and got all worked up until...[*Pause. He moves to the suitcase and materials.*] So here we go.

QUEENY. It's the start, Johnny...the clean start. Yours as well as mine. And I still say they look like the rainbow.

JOHNNY [*picking up one piece of material*]. The colours are good...

QUEENY [*mimicking his sales talk*]. And they won't run.

JOHNNY [*laughing*]. Maybe you should also sell.

QUEENY. Not today...I got to prepare for our celebration.

JOHNNY. I'd better start selling and give us something to celebrate. [*As they get down to business, the old enthusiasm comes back slowly.*] I'm not going to take it all...just a few pieces. We'll see how it goes with them. If I need the others I'll come back.

QUEENY. You got the address of the two women?

JOHNNY. Right here.

QUEENY. What time do you think you'll be back?

JOHNNY. About five.

QUEENY. If I'm not here just make yourself at home.

JOHNNY. While you're about it, find out the price of a good sewing machine...who knows.

[*The door opens and Sam comes in.*]

QUEENY [*Watching him inspect the materials*]. Well? [*A note of triumph in her voice.*]

93

SAM [*giving Queeny a quick look but directing his attention to Johnny*]
So you mean to try it?

QUEENY [*pointing to materials*]. Would that be here if we wasn't?

JOHNNY. That's about it. You look doubtful.

QUEENY. It's a bad habit Sam's got. He doubts everything.

SAM. What you reckon you're going to make on that?

JOHNNY. About fifty per cent if I'm lucky.

SAM. Not much, is it?

QUEENY. It's not a racket, Sam, it's legitimate business.

SAM [*ignoring Queeny*]. Are you lucky?

JOHNNY. No more than anybody else.

SAM. Looks to me like you got a lot of luck

JOHNNY. We'll see at the end of today.

SAM. We seen a lot already. Yesterday you didn't even know Queen
and today you're in business with her! Ten quid's worth
business. I call that luck.

JOHNNY. Maybe I am.

SAM. You bet you are.

JOHNNY. Anyway I got to be off now...see if my luck still hold
good. See you later, Queeny.

QUEENY. Five o'clock, Johnny.

[*Johnny exits carrying his suitcase. Sam helps himself to a drink an
then sits down.*]

SAM. So I was wrong.

QUEENY. Looks like it, doesn't it?

SAM. Maybe he's playing for more than even I thought.

QUEENY. Meaning?

SAM. You're worth a lot more than ten pounds.

QUEENY [*coming forward*]. Sam, I want you to listen carefully, 'caus
I never said anything I meant so much...He can have it...he ca
have every penny I got.

SAM. Is it that bad?

QUEENY. Bad? That I found somebody who's worth giving to? It
good, Sam. It feels good. I'm going to enjoy waking up in t
morning.

SAM. I do that for nothing.

QUEENY. For nothing or the cheapest! That's you, that's been yo ever since I can remember. And now I feel sorry for you. *Ja*, I actually feel sorry. Yesterday I said I envied you 'cause you had the shop and I just sat around and did nothing. It's changed, Sam, in one day it's changed, and you know how? You've got nobody...

SAM. And you've got Johnny.

QUEENY. That's it.

SAM. It's not much if you have a good look at it.

QUEENY. Why you scared, Sam?

SAM. Me?

QUEENY. There's only me and you and I'm not talking to myself. Yes, scared. You're working on him like a man that's scared.

SAM. You're talking nonsense.

QUEENY. You didn't laugh, Sam. If I was wrong you would have laughed.

SAM. What have I got to be scared about?

QUEENY. I don't know and I'm not interested in finding out. You just look scared. I know I'm not.

SAM. We'll see how long it lasts.

QUEENY. It will last as long as it's got to.

SAM. He might not be the settling-down type, Queeny.

QUEENY. Could be, but I'll try and make it that he wants to. But like you said we don't know. I do know this though, if anybody tries to interfere they'll wish they was never born.

SAM. Don't look at me. If you get a kick out of it good luck to you. All I'm saying is he might decide to drift and when he does you'll be glad you still got the shebeen going.

QUEENY. That's finished.

SAM. What do you mean?

QUEENY. What I said. The shebeen is finished. I'm in a legitimate business and it's going to stay that way.

SAM. Are you mad?

QUEENY. Don't shout.

SAM. Legitimate business? Selling rags?

QUEENY. That's how we're starting.

SAM. Starting what? You think you'll ever pick up two hundred per cent profit selling rags? Because that's what you get from the shebeen. And you don't have to work for it.

QUEENY. That's just what I don't like.

SAM. Then keep your rag-bag as a side line.

QUEENY. I'm keeping it, don't worry about that, but it's all I'm keeping.

SAM. So you mean to wreck everything.

QUEENY. What is there to wreck, Sam? You just show me one decent thing that I got to wreck.

SAM. The best shebeen in town...the best customers...

QUEENY [cutting him short]. I said 'decent'. Go read somewhere what that word means. You're the one that's been to school, remember you just picked me up in the gutter.

SAM. And I'll be doing that again if you carry on like this. That boy's going to take a powder with all you got and then you'll be back there looking for Sam to pick you up.

QUEENY. Don't.

SAM. Wait till the boys hear about this tonight.

QUEENY. They won't. I'm not selling. I said it's finished and I'm starting from now.

SAM. And that liquor I got?

QUEENY. The liquor *I* bought. I don't give a damn. It can stay here for the rest of my life as far as I'm concerned. Tonight we're going to celebrate.

SAM. Celebrate?

QUEENY. Yes, celebrate! Me and Johnny, right here. 'The boys' can go somewhere else, go moan and vomit on somebody else's floor 'cause I'm finished with it. I'm going to start to live, Sam.

SAM. That's funny...coming from you.

QUEENY. Meaning?

SAM. Nothing.

QUEENY. Don't be scared. I got a lot to remember and one of the things is that no one ever really treated me like a woman, took their hat off when they came in here, said please or thank you or said they liked my smile. I remember that all right, and I remember you. You got fat and rich and smooth on me. You worked me like men work horses and it lasted a long time, so long that I forgot I was a woman. I took this whole Goddamn city to bed with me so that you could get fat and rich. I also made money out of it . . . I remember that too, but it's money I don't like the feel of. It's a greasy coin that stinks of dirty sheets and unwashed men. So if I want to give it away, if I want to give away every penny I got, I don't think I should be ashamed. [*Pause.*] I'm going out now, Sam. When I come back it's going to be my home 'cause that's what it is and that's the way you and everybody else is going to treat it.

[*Queeny leaves. Sam sits meditatively with his glass for a time. Then the door opens and Blackie comes in, still carrying his clock.*]

BLACKIE. Where's Queeny?

SAM. How the hell must I know.

BLACKIE [*seeing the material*]. This chap come?

SAM. Do you think that walked in here by itself?

BLACKIE [*speaking to himself*]. It's no good.

SAM. What do you say?

BLACKIE. It's no good.

SAM [*on the point of making another cutting remark when he stops and picks his words carefully*]. What do you mean?

BLACKIE. This fellow.

SAM. Don't you like him?

BLACKIE. If he comes, I must go.

SAM. You're right and it's all wrong. He doesn't mean any good. He only wants Queeny's money.

BLACKIE. He's no good.

SAM. It would be better if he went.

BLACKIE. Queeny likes him.

SAM. I know but she doesn't see him the way we do. [*Pause.*] You want to get rid of him, Blackie.

BLACKIE. Queeny would be angry.

SAM. I don't mean you must get rough with him. You needn't touch him at all.

BLACKIE. No?

SAM. You needn't lay a hand on him.

BLACKIE. How?

[*Sam goes to the door and sees nobody is listening. He closes it and joins Blackie at the table.*]

SAM. Listen carefully . . .

CURTAIN

Scene 2

Queeny's shebeen that afternoon. Sam is sitting at the table deep in thought. Blackie is prowling around at the back, obviously nervous. He goes to the window every few seconds and looks out into the street.

SAM [*looking up irritably*]. Why don't you sit down?

BLACKIE. I can't.

SAM. Then do something. Wind your clock if you want to hear the damn thing again. But stop crawling around. It gets on my nerves.

BLACKIE. I don't like it.

SAM. What you worrying about? I fixed it so that she will never know it was us.

BLACKIE. Yes.

SAM. Patrick does the dirty work.

BLACKIE. Maybe he will tell Queeny.

SAM. Tell her what? Don't be a fool. I paid him and I said I'll help him get a job. So Queeny never sells to him again. He can get his liquor somewhere else. And she won't worry about doing Patrick if I tell her you beat him up. So make it look good. But remember it's only got to look good. Go easy on Patrick. He's doing this because we asked him.

BLACKIE. [*After a few seconds of pacing another thought has struck him.*] She'll want to know how Patrick found out about her.

SAM [*explaining very carefully*]. That woman took on more men in her day than you'll ever know. So one of them saw Queeny around and tells Patrick, one of her old customers. Isn't that possible? [*Blackie nods his head in grudging agreement. Sam settles back comfortably to enjoy the cunning of his plan.*]

I must give it to myself, it's tidy: Not a loophole. I used what they call psychology. That for your benefit is the head and I been using mine. I could have got somebody to take him down a dark street... you might have done it for a price. But that's messy and the police could get round to asking questions. But this way it's me and you and Patrick and each of us got a good reason to shut up.

BLACKIE. Maybe it doesn't work. Maybe this fellow won't care about what Queeny was.

SAM. He will. He's the type. The fastidious kind, that don't like chewing on a bone after all the other dogs taken the meat off.

BLACKIE. I don't like you, Sam.

SAM [*with sarcasm*]. Don't let that worry you. All that's important is that we don't like him.

BLACKIE [*showing his reluctance to implement Sam's plan*]. Maybe I'm wrong, about this chap. Queeny said he was all right.

SAM [*quick to react*]. You mad or something? I explained to you how this chap is going to steal Queeny's cash, didn't I? How you was going to be kicked out because he's come?

[*Blackie is not completely convinced.*]

Look, if I had told you yesterday, just yesterday, that Queeny was going to close up this shebeen, would you have believed me? No. But she has. In one day this Johnny bloke has got her so wrapped up that she's done that.

Queeny uses you around the shebeen. You fetch liquor, you throw out the drunks. But what are you going to do in this cloth business? Sew on curtain rings? And remember we are doing this to protect Queeny.

[*Blackie paces again.*]

So take it easy. This chap is no fool and he'll quickly smell a rat. You got nothing to be nervous about. You're not going to hurt him. Queeny won't be home till late so we got plenty of time. When he comes I'll go across and give Patrick the word. If everything goes right tonight will be the last we'll see of that bastard.

BLACKIE. Why don't you like him?

SAM. I don't like him cause he's going to steal Queeny's cash. [*That was for Blackie's benefit. The next few words in a more introspective mood.*] And because he's a fancy boy. A straight man that makes like everything else is crooked. Wait till he hears about Queeny.

BLACKIE. Here he comes.

SAM [*joining him at the window*]. He looks happy.

BLACKIE. Must have sold the lot.

SAM. So he was lucky today. That is where it ends. Keep him busy till I come back.

[*Sam hurriedly exits through the shut door. Blackie, left alone, shows a moment of panic. He looks around uncertainly for something to do. He sees his clock, goes over to it, and starts winding. The door opens*

99

and Johnny comes in.]

JOHNNY. Hello! Where's Queeny?

BLACKIE. Be here just now.

[*Johnny sits down. He is obviously excited and elated.*]

JOHNNY. I sold everything I had with me.

BLACKIE. *Ja.*

JOHNNY. I reckon that's pretty good going.

BLACKIE. Maybe.

JOHNNY. I think so. I mean it's not something that people got t
buy. Like soap or medicine. But they bought it. Rags or not the
bought every piece I had. And you know I could have sold th
lot . . . I mean the stuff I left behind as well. Hey . . . what abou
you?

BLACKIE. What about me?

JOHNNY. Wouldn't you like to come out with me next time and giv
a hand with the selling? You'd get paid. You do sort of hel
Queeny with things, don't you? It's her money that started thi
It's her business as well.

BLACKIE. Me?

JOHNNY. Why not? Looks like I'm going to need somebody. Migl
as well keep it in the family.

BLACKIE [*confused*]. I don't know nothing about selling.

JOHNNY. I didn't when I started this morning. It's what you wa
to do, Blackie . . .

BLACKIE [*trying to kill the doubts in his mind*]. No!

JOHNNY. Of course you can if you try.

BLACKIE. I said no. I don't even want to try.

JOHNNY [*misinterpreting Blackie's refusal*]. Look, I bet . . .

BLACKIE [*turning on him*]. I don't want to sell your bloody rags. S
shut up.

[*Blackie moves to the door but is a few seconds too late. Sam
there.*]

SAM [*sauntering over and dropping into a chair beside Johnny*]. Ho
did it go?

JOHNNY. Okay.

SAM. Just okay or okay fine?

JOHNNY. I sold the lot.

SAM. The lot. That's good going.

JOHNNY. I'm glad, for Queeny's sake. She took a chance giving me ten quid like that.

SAM. Chance?

JOHNNY. The material.

SAM. Oh, that.

JOHNNY [*detecting an undercurrent in Sam's words*]. Well, didn't she?

SAM. Sure, but don't get all worked up about it. Ten pounds is small change to that woman. I don't think she worried too much about that.

JOHNNY. Meaning?

SAM. Maybe she has other ideas. That's all. What did you take?

JOHNNY. The eight pounds I spent on the material and four pounds profit.

SAM. Not bad. What do you say, Blackie? Don't tell me, I know. Queeny's not interested in chicken feed.

JOHNNY. I think she will be.

SAM [*winking at him*]. I get you.

JOHNNY. What do you mean?

SAM. Nothing. Maybe I known Queeny a little longer than you. [*There is a vigorous knock at the door.*]

SAM. See who it is, Blackie. And remember what Queeny said. She's not selling tonight. [*He turns to Johnny.*] That's right, isn't it?

[*Blackie goes to the door and talks to someone outside. Voices get loud and then Patrick comes in.*]

PATRICK [*to Sam*]. Tell him I don't want credit. I got money. [*He sits down.*] How's everybody?

SAM [*ignoring the greeting*]. Blackie wasn't talking about credit. Queeny's not selling.

PATRICK. Look, where is she?

SAM. Not in.

PATRICK. I'm sorry about last night. I didn't mean to mess up her place.

SAM. It's got nothing to do with last night. [*Turning to Johnny.*] Isn't that so?

PATRICK. Well then why isn't she selling?

SAM. She said something about celebrating. Anyway it's not your business.

PATRICK. With all the cash she's taken from me it could be.

SAM. Be a good boy and take your few pennies elsewhere, huh.

PATRICK. Few pennies. So my money's not good enough for her any more.

SAM. I just said she's not selling.

PATRICK. It was good enough for her when she first came here. My few pennies were all right then. I bet they were. Because I earned my money honest. Not like some people I know.

SAM. Don't say anything you're going to regret.

PATRICK. I got no regrets. I got nothing to hide.

JOHNNY. What do you mean by that?

PATRICK. Hell, you must be new here to ask questions like that. Go ask Queeny.

JOHNNY. I'm asking you.

SAM. Look, let's just forget what has been said . . .

JOHNNY [*to Patrick*]. I'm asking you, what has Queeny got to hide?

SAM. You'll be sorry, Patrick.

PATRICK. Sorry? Sorry for what. I've got nothing to be ashamed of. I lived my life clean and decent.

SAM. Blackie!

[*The hunchback rushes forward and lifting his clenched fists cracks them into Patrick's back. Sam sees that Blackie is not bluffing, that he has every intention of killing Patrick. He rushes in and pulls Blackie off. Johnny is riveted to his chair by Patrick's insinuations.*]

SAM. You fool. You bloody crooked fool. Do you want to kill him?

BLACKIE. Yes.

SAM. Listen! That's enough. That's enough. Do you hear?

[*Blackie is brought to his senses. He gives up the struggle with Patrick and rushes out of the room. Sam turns to Patrick.*]

You all right?

[*Patrick nods his head. He is shaken and Sam helps him to the door and slips something into his hand before he goes. Sam takes out a handkerchief and mops his brow before turning his attention to Johnny.*]

SAM. Thanks for the help.

JOHNNY [*ignoring the sarcasm*]. What did he mean?

SAM. How must I know? You saw him last night. Drinks a lot. Must have had a few tots somewhere else before coming here.

JOHNNY. He was sober. You've known Queeny a long time. What did she do before...?

SAM. Look, I told you I don't know. And even if I did what sort of friend goes talking behind a back? If Queeny wants you to know, let her tell you.

JOHNNY. Know what?

SAM. I know nothing, absolutely nothing. Does that make you understand? I'm keeping my mouth shut. Anyway here she comes now. And if you want my advice don't ask questions.

[*Sam exits quietly through the shut door. Johnny waits nervously for Queeny to appear.*]

QUEENY [*entering loaded with parcels*]. Can we celebrate?

JOHNNY. Hello, Queeny.

QUEENY. How did it go?

JOHNNY. It was good.

QUEENY [*her excitement getting the better of her*]. No!

JOHNNY. Yep, the lot.

QUEENY. Everything you took out?

JOHNNY. Everything.

QUEENY. We've done it! We can celebrate...and I *mean* celebrate. [*She shows her parcels.*] Fancy candles for the table...a new set of knives and forks...a chicken...Got to see if I can still cook one. And you know what this is? Champagne...the real thing. I even bought myself a new dress.
[*She pauses.*] Don't look at me like that. Am I making a fool of myself?

JOHNNY. No, Queeny.

QUEENY. What if I was! I got good reason to stand in the door there and laugh at this damn street till the dogs get tired of barking. Aren't you happy?

JOHNNY. Tired, I guess.

QUEENY. Of course. It must have been hard work. I'll put the kettle on. Don't fiddle with the parcels. There's a surprise for you. Johnny, it's hard for me to believe this has been a day in my life...shopping, arguing prices. You know I argued with an

Indian about the price of potatoes. And this was the one I hated most of all. Pay day. The big money day. When life started at night and sobered up two hangovers and a hundred brandies later on Monday. Fifteen years is a long time.

JOHNNY. Fifteen? This morning you said five.

QUEENY. Five, of course. What's the matter with me?

[*Picks up one of the parcels.*] Look the other way.

[*A new dress comes out of the parcel. She starts to put it on.*]

JOHNNY. What did you do before this, Queeny?

QUEENY. Just knocked about. Odd jobs.

JOHNNY. Queeny.

QUEENY. *Ja.*

JOHNNY. I need a drink.

QUEENY. Shall we open the champagne now?

JOHNNY. Let's keep that for later. What about brandy?

QUEENY. You asking for brandy.

JOHNNY. I'm all jumpy inside.

QUEENY. I understand. It's in the kitchen in the cupboard. Help yourself.

[*Johnny, still not looking at Queeny, goes into the kitchen and returns with a bottle. He opens it and pours himself a drink which he drinks down, standing in the doorway, then another which he brings into the room with the bottle. Queeny has now finished putting on the new dress.*]

QUEENY. Well, how do you like it?

JOHNNY. It looks good.

QUEENY. Now tell me. Tell me everything that happened to you from the moment you left this morning.

JOHNNY. Well, it's hard. Everything is mixed up. I went to those women I told you about. After that I just kept on going and when I looked again my suitcases was empty. Here, see for yourself. The eight pounds I spent on material plus four pounds profit. That's not bad. Even Sam said so.

QUEENY. I can laugh at him today. Let's call him over.

JOHNNY. No. Leave him alone. I don't like his company, or his talk.

QUEENY. You haven't told me all. Did they buy like you suggested? Table cloths to match the curtains and so on?

JOHNNY. *Ja*. I reckon so.

QUEENY. What's the matter, Johnny? You're not burning up the world like you were this morning.

JOHNNY. Somebody threw cold water on the fire.

QUEENY. I don't get you.

JOHNNY. Well, you know, selling and arguing about prices. It makes you tired.

QUEENY. You look more than just tired.

JOHNNY [*covering up*]. Don't worry, I'll have the fire burning bright again. [*Pours himself another drink*.]

QUEENY. I'll get the coffee. You might really need it. [*The last remark as a joke with a gesture towards the brandy*.]

[*Queeny goes out to the kitchen. Johnny downs the tot. With his face screwed up and his throat burning he puts out his hand for the bottle and pours another*.]

QUEENY [*from the other room*]. What do we do now?

JOHNNY. We said celebrate, didn't we?

QUEENY [*in the doorway*]. You're sounding like your old self again. Maybe that brandy was a good idea. But I meant the business. What do we do now? Buy some more?

JOHNNY. We expand.

QUEENY. Expand?

JOHNNY. We get big. It's when you're small and need people that you get buggered around. We've got to be so big we don't need anybody.

QUEENY. Except each other.

JOHNNY. Except each other? Maybe we'll still be buggered around, by each other. I suppose the only time you're really safe is when you can tell the rest of the world to go to hell.

QUEENY. That's not true. Remember me when you say that. Nothing buggers you up like yourself. It's good to need someone. [*Trying to change the subject*.] Tell me about our expansion.

JOHNNY. We'll buy more, sell more, and make more money. Then you'll start taking it serious.

QUEENY [*not understanding his last remark*]. Johnny?

JOHNNY. Four pounds *is* chicken feed, isn't it?

QUEENY. Who said that?

JOHNNY. Blackie.

QUEENY. He said that ... about me?

JOHNNY. Let's forget it.

QUEENY. No! Not if you're going to believe everything you hear ..

JOHNNY. I didn't say I believed it.

QUEENY. What else did he say?

JOHNNY. Queeny, please.

QUEENY. So that is what I get after all I did for him ...

JOHNNY. He's not ungrateful, Queeny.

QUEENY. I should have known it.

JOHNNY. I offered him a job.

QUEENY. Doing what?

JOHNNY. Helping me.

QUEENY. Well, drop that idea.

JOHNNY. Why?

QUEENY. Because I don't think it's a good idea to have him around

JOHNNY. So you'll just get rid of him like that?

QUEENY. Just like that. That's how he came and that's how he can go

JOHNNY. And when you get tired of selling rags will I also go just
like that?
[*Queeny is disturbed.*]

QUEENY. Johnny, we're going wrong.

JOHNNY. You're right [*pulling himself together*].
[*He takes the bottle and pours himself another drink.*]

QUEENY. Easy on that stuff, Johnny. You're not used to it.

JOHNNY. You want me to burn again, don't you?

QUEENY. We got the future to burn up. Tomorrow and the day after
and our plans for those days. That stuff will only burn you up.

JOHNNY. The fire needs a spark. That's all this is giving me. Now
about these plans. They got to be big. We got to get away from
a world that is small. We got to build big so that one of these days
we can stand in the street and have a damned good laughing session
at the world. We'll laugh ourselves sick 'cause there's nothing so
Goddamn funny only we take it serious.

QUEENY [*trying hard to bring him back to reality*]. The plans, Johnny

JOHNNY. Plans?

QUEENY. You started off saying you wanted to talk about our plans for the future.

JOHNNY. The future! It's a waste of time talking about that. The only future we've got is tomorrow if we're unlucky enough to wake up.

QUEENY [*still trying*]. I got the prices of sewing machines. I was thinking that for us...

JOHNNY. Sewing machines!

QUEENY. You said we got to get a sewing machine, Johnny. I got the prices in my bag.

JOHNNY. Forget the sewing machine. That's a small thought.

QUEENY. I heard big talkers all my life, but I never seen one that was happy. And you were happy this morning, Johnny.

JOHNNY. I'm happy now.

QUEENY. Are you?

JOHNNY [*passing a hand over his eyes*]. I told you I'm tired.

QUEENY. Is it because of what you told me this morning?

JOHNNY. No. I want to forget that tonight.

QUEENY [*pointing to the bottle*]. That's not the way.

JOHNNY. I still got to find that out for myself.

[*Queeny picks up her parcels and takes them to the kitchen. A few seconds later she returns with a small one in her hands.*]

QUEENY. I should have given this to you when I came in. When I was all excited.

[*There is a pause. Queeny is embarrassed.*]

It's a present for you, Johnny. Hell, I'm just making a fool of myself. [*She moves to the back.*]

JOHNNY. Queeny...

QUEENY [*stopping*]. Maybe you will like it.

[*She gives it to him. He opens the parcel and takes out a wristwatch.*]

It's just a wristwatch. I thought that maybe when you was going around selling and it comes near lunch...[*Her words trail off.*] I just wanted to give you something. It doesn't mean anything else.

[*Johnny goes to the back. A shadow passes the window. It is a man picking out a melancholy little theme on his guitar. Johnny hears the music.*]

JOHNNY [*with a vague gesture towards the window*]. Him.

QUEENY. Who?

JOHNNY. The chap who was playing the guitar.

QUEENY [*listening*]. It's sad.

JOHNNY. It's always sad. When a man walks past a lighted window in an empty street, it's always sad.

QUEENY. Why has it got to be?

JOHNNY. When you're out walking at this hour streets lead nowhere

QUEENY. You don't have to say it like that.

JOHNNY. It's true.

QUEENY. For you?

JOHNNY. I don't know myself any more.

QUEENY. I know a few things.

JOHNNY. I told you a lot.

QUEENY. I'm not talking about that. I'm talking about a man I me yesterday who got his chance to do something he's been dreaming of for a long time. A man who's got big plans for the future Doesn't that sound like somebody who's got somewhere to go?

JOHNNY. I seen good-looking apples with worms in them.

QUEENY. What do you mean?

JOHNNY. The apple isn't going to get ripe. And even if it looks like it is, the first person that takes a bite will spit it out . . . because they'll find it rotten inside. It only takes one worm to do that to an apple . . . and maybe one thought to do it to a man. [*Johnny turns and looks directly at Queeny.*] And you?

QUEENY. I'm trying to be a woman.

JOHNNY. What does that mean?

QUEENY. I'm trying to hold a man, make him want to stay.

JOHNNY [*after a pause*]. Am I the first?

QUEENY [*choosing her words very carefully*]. It's the first time I've ever felt like this about someone.

[*Johnny wants to ask something else. The evasion is obvious but he is no yet drunk enough to force Queeny. He pours himself another drink just a little too hurriedly. Queeny watches his hands and the glass.*]

JOHNNY. Must have been a harder day than I thought.

[*There is a knock at the door. Queeny answers it. It is a customer and she has difficulty in telling him she is not selling. She steps back into the room and slams the door.*]

JOHNNY. It's not going to be easy.

QUEENY. What?

JOHNNY. Keeping it shut. They're going to expect you to sell.

QUEENY. What they expect and what I'm going to do is two different things.

JOHNNY. Looks like it.

QUEENY. I thought you would prefer it this way, Johnny.

JOHNNY. There's worse things in this world than shebeens.

QUEENY. I closed it because it's the only thing you or anybody else can point at in my life.

JOHNNY. You don't have to say that.

QUEENY. Don't I?

JOHNNY. We said we were going to celebrate, remember.

QUEENY. We've gone a long way from that idea.

JOHNNY [*Pause.*] Why did you get mixed up with a bastard like me?

QUEENY. Don't blame yourself, Johnny.

JOHNNY. Then don't blame yourself either. Let's blame the stinking bloody world out there that makes us what we are. Let's blame what sent us into this world because nobody with any sense would choose to come.

QUEENY. Is that how you feel about it?

JOHNNY. I've felt that way ever since the mines. Ever since they got hold of me and made me worse than an animal. The only difference is that sometimes I get the crazy idea that a man can change the world he lives in. Hell! You can't even change yourself. [*Grabbing the bottle.*] Except that this isn't helping me forget.

QUEENY. Have a cup of coffee instead.

JOHNNY. Who ever heard of celebrating with coffee?

QUEENY. I'd rather not celebrate than see you start on that.

JOHNNY. Don't sell me that line.

QUEENY. Then there's no point in me turning them away at the door.

JOHNNY. This is my last one.

QUEENY. Promise.

JOHNNY. Please, Queeny, don't nag. There's the money we took today, if that's what you're worrying about. [*He shows it to her. Pause.*] I'm sorry.

QUEENY. Is that something else Blackie said and you believed? [*Moving to the door.*] Where is he?

JOHNNY. No! Queeny, please. [*She stops at the door.*] Christ, this is one hell of a way to celebrate.

[*There is a knock at the door. Queeny ignores it. It comes again. she opens the door in a fury.*]

QUEENY [*to the person outside*]. Go to hell. [*She slams the door.*] Let's try to start from the beginning.

JOHNNY. The beginning. Where's that?

QUEENY. Two hours ago when you come home. You had sold everything and you were tired. Be tired, too tired to say anything or think anything. Just want to sit down and rest and wait for the food. Maybe later we'll have some of that champagne.

JOHNNY [*genuinely exhausted*]. That sounds simple. That sounds simple and okay.

QUEENY. Try it, Johnny. Sit down. Or do you want to sleep?

JOHNNY. No, sometimes a man can dream worse things than he can think. There was a time when I couldn't sleep at all, because of my dreams.

QUEENY. It's okay now, Johnny.

JOHNNY. It wasn't then. No. I'll stay awake. It feels like a night for bad dreams.

QUEENY. Dream about today.

JOHNNY. How do you know what today means to me?

QUEENY. You sold everything . . .

JOHNNY. Don't keep on about that like it was the happy ending to a fairy story. So I sold a heap of old rags. But I didn't sell my mind. I still got the same thoughts. I'm the same man as yesterday and the day before that right back to the mines. I never sold myself and bought a brand new person. [*Pause.*] Here we go again. You make the supper. I'll be okay.

[*Queeny goes to the kitchen. Johnny prowls around nervously. The shadow of the man with the guitar passes the window again. We hear the music. It seems to drive Johnny to the point of desperation. He rushes to the window.*]

[*Queeny comes back. Johnny sees the bottle of champagne.*]

JOHNNY. Let's have the champagne now.

QUEENY. Go ahead.

[*While Johnny works out the cork, she fetches two glasses. Johnny drinks his straight down.*]

QUEENY. Aren't we supposed to touch the glasses together?

JOHNNY. Of course, I forgot. [*Pours himself another glass.*] To ourselves, since nobody else gives a damn.

QUEENY. To ourselves and the business.
[*There is a knock at the door.*]

JOHNNY. Can't you stop that damned knocking?

QUEENY. The only way I can do that is to leave the door open and let them come in.
[*The knock comes again.*]

JOHNNY. Well, answer it, tell him to go to hell like you did the others, but shut him up.

QUEENY. You're shouting.
[*We hear the knock again.*]

JOHNNY. Okay, I'm shouting...but it's because that's getting on my nerves.
[*Queeny goes across and opens the door.*]

QUEENY. Nobody here.

JOHNNY. You don't keep customers by keeping them waiting.

QUEENY. Then I'd better not answer the door.

JOHNNY. You sure you want to lose them?

QUEENY. Meaning?

JOHNNY. Next Friday you might think it better business to open again.

QUEENY. Why should I want to do that?
[*Johnny is saved from answering by another knock at the door.*]

JOHNNY. Christ, there it goes again.

QUEENY. You didn't answer my question.

JOHNNY. If you'll tell him to shut up.

QUEENY. I asked you ...

JOHNNY. Well, stop asking me...You might get an answer you...
[*He moves suddenly and knocks over the bottle of champagne. It spills over the table cloth, then drips onto the floor. They watch as if mesmerized. The knocking is heard again.*]

QUEENY. I told Sam I was closing down because I was sick of drunks messing up my place. [*She speaks quietly.*]

JOHNNY [*moving suddenly*]. I need some fresh air.

QUEENY. Johnny!

JOHNNY [*a cry of desperation*]. The window ... I'm only going to the window ... Don't suffocate me, Queeny ...

QUEENY. What's happening, Johnny? What's gone wrong?

[*Pause. Johnny gets a grip on himself.*]

JOHNNY. I got the smell of filth again. Queeny, I wanted to start today more than anything else in my life. I thought I'd been given my chance to start from the beginning ... I want to do that ... Jesus knows, I want to do that. I told you about myself this morning, Queeny. It wasn't just that I owed you a start ... I looked at you like I've never looked at another woman before ... I don't want to run away from it but ... Queeny, I been honest with you ... you got to be honest with me. But tell me ... I got to know ...

QUEENY. Who ...?

JOHNNY. Queeny, listen ...

QUEENY. Who told you?

JOHNNY. Nobody told me anything.

QUEENY. Blackie!

JOHNNY. He didn't say a thing.

QUEENY. It was Blackie.

JOHNNY. If you go out without telling me, I won't be here when you come back.

QUEENY. Why must you know?

JOHNNY. I got to stop myself thinking.

QUEENY. Will it make any difference what I tell you?

JOHNNY. Don't ask me that. I'm not God. I didn't make myself.

QUEENY. I didn't ask you any questions about yourself.

JOHNNY. Can't you see, Queeny, I had to tell you, just like I got to know now?

QUEENY. But you're asking me. You're asking me for something I've been trying to hide away from myself. Give me time, Johnny. Give me time to live with myself and find the right words, and tell you when I know I got to, when I can.

JOHNNY. And what must I do?

QUEENY. Wait. You got to wait.

JOHNNY. Wait. You know what that word means ... wait? That

means days, weeks, months, maybe years. I just had two hours of it and it's driving me mad. And you know why? Because you don't stop thinking when you're waiting. [*Pause.*] Queeny, let me go. Let me walk out of that door.

QUEENY. No.

JOHNNY. If I stay I got to know.

QUEENY. You said this morning . . .

JOHNNY. Don't stall, Queeny! Tell me or let me go.

[*Evasions are past. Queeny realizes that she can no longer avoid the truth.*]

QUEENY. Where do I begin?

JOHNNY. There is a name for everything.

QUEENY. Nongogo.

JOHNNY. Jesus!

QUEENY. Yes . . . Nongogo . . . a woman for two and six. Don't you think that was a bargain? Me for two and six. And you're seeing me when I'm older and fat. You should have seen me then . . . Maybe you would have joined the queue.

JOHNNY. No.

QUEENY. Yes . . . I'm telling you yes.

JOHNNY. Stop it.

QUEENY. You wanted to know so I'm telling you, Johnny, and now you got to listen. I did it because I was hungry, because I had sworn to myself I was going to make enough to tell the rest of the world to go to hell. And nothing makes money like Sam organizing the business. We started with queues around the mine dumps at night. I can also tell you a few things about compounds, Johnny. But we ended big . . . one man at a time. That's how I got here and Sam got his shop across the street and that's the ten pounds that bought you rags and the first decent thing I've ever had in my life. Because if you think I liked it or wanted it that way you're so far away from knowing what a woman is, you can forget them. I'm a woman, Johnny. I never stopped being one, but no one's given me a chance. I've had men but never one who treated me like I mattered far more than just a night in bed. Because that man I'll love. If he'll just take me, for what I want to be and not what I was. I'll make him happy. God's been generous in what he's given me. In body, in feelings, in the need for love ... give me a chance ...

JOHNNY. Stop using words that mean nothing. Love, chance ... God made me without the one and my life's had nothing of the other. Why didn't you say you were filth ... like me? When I walked in here last night, why didn't you recognize another piece of trash? Why did I have to think you were different?

QUEENY. Different from what? The respectable people out there? Respectable? They were my customers ... the ones that lived cleanest and hated filth ... like you! I've found Bibles in their pockets when they lay sleeping in my bed, with pictures of their pretty wives and nice clean children. And I bet Daddy took them all to church on Sundays.

JOHNNY. Don't drag everything into the gutter with you, Queeny.

QUEENY. I'm not the landlord of that strip of muck, Johnny. Everybody owns a plot down there.

JOHNNY. Some of us try to crawl out of it.

QUEENY. What do you think I've been doing for five years? It had ended, Johnny, it was dead and buried when you walked in here. But you won't let it stay that way, will you? You'd be worse than Sam, who just sighs when he passes the grave. You've dug it up. You've performed a miracle, Johnny. The miracle of Jesus and the dead body. You've brought it back to life. The warmth of your hate, the breath of your disgust has got it living again. I'm not too old ... not *too* fat ... even you looked at me like you never looked at another woman. God's put a lot of men onto this earth. There are a lot of streets I haven't walked, lamposts I haven't stood under, faces I haven't smiled at.

[*Hands on her hips, she starts laughing at Johnny and walks up to him provocatively. He turns and goes out, with Queeny laughing loudly. When Johnny has gone, Queeny goes to the door, flings it open, and shouts out into the street.*]

QUEENY. Where's everybody? This damn place is a graveyard. I've got a locker full of booze and it's not diluted.

[*Queeny goes back into the room. She goes to the mirror, puts on lipstick ... rouge ... earrings ... bracelets, and dolls herself up into the real tart.*]

SAM [*appearing at the door*]. Did I hear right?

QUEENY. What did you hear, Sam?

SAM. I heard something that sounded like the old Queeny.

QUEENY. There's nothing wrong with your hearing.
  [*Sam laughs. He goes back into the street.*]

SAM [*off stage*]. Come on . . . I'm telling you it's all right.
  [*Sam comes back rubbing his hands.*]

SAM. We still got time. It's only nine. When the word gets around
  that Queeny's back in business, they'll be back for the ball.
  [*Patrick enters hesitantly.*]

SAM. Come in.

PATRICK. Is this on the level?

QUEENY. The only level we worry about here is that in the brandy
  bottle. Where's Blackie? Blackie!

SAM [*to Patrick*]. Didn't I tell you?

PATRICK. You sure did.

QUEENY. What did you call the kid, Patrick?

PATRICK. Kid? It was twins.
  [*Blackie appears.*]

QUEENY. Where have you been? I got customers and you're keeping
  them waiting.
  [*Blackie backs away uncertainly . . . Sam and Patrick laugh at the
  expression on his face.*]

QUEENY [*pouring the rest of the champagne*]. Have some of this while
  you're waiting.

PATRICK. What is it?

SAM. Champagne.

PATRICK. Lemonade!

SAM. You got no taste.
  [*Blackie has brought in the liquor.*]

SAM [*pours the drinks*]. You had us worried.

PATRICK. You sure did.

SAM. It's like old times again.

PATRICK. It sure is. What happened to that salesman, Queeny?

QUEENY. Man. There was no man here.

CURTAIN

NO-GOOD FRIDAY

The play is set in SOPHIA TOWN, an African township near Johannes-burg.

Scene 1—A backyard on a Friday night
Scene 2—The same, an hour later
Scene 3—Willie's room the following Sunday night
Scene 4—The same, Friday night five days later
Scene 5—The backyard a few minutes later

CHARACTERS

REBECCA	a young woman living with Willie Seopela
GUY	jazz musician and friend of Willie's
WATSON	a township politician
WILLIE	a man in his thirties
FATHER HIGGINS	a White priest
TOBIAS	an African from the rural areas visiting Johannesburg for the first time
PINKIE PETER	backyard characters
MOSES	a blind man
SHARK	a township gangster
HARRY	one of his thugs
A SECOND THUG	

This play was given its first performance in August 1958 at the Bantu-mens Social Centre with Athol Fugard as Higgins, Bloke Modisane a Shark, and Lewis Nkosi as Willie. Its first performance outside Sout Africa was at the Crucible Studio, Sheffield, on 6 November 1974 with th following cast:

Rebecca	*Merdeue Jordine*
Guy	*Jimi Rand*
Watson	*Nik Abraham*
Willie	*Alton Kumalo*
Higgins	*Iain Armstrong*
Tobias	*Christopher Asante*
Pinkie	*Salami Coker*
Peter	*Nik Abraham*
Moses	*Tommy Buson*
Shark	*Lloyd Anderson*
Harry	*Joseph Iles*

SCENE ONE

A backyard in Sophia Town, late Friday afternoon. Clustered about it are a few rusty corrugated-iron shacks. Rebecca, *a young woman in her early twenties, is taking down washing from a line strung between a fence and one of the houses. A few other women drift in and out of doors preparing for the return of their men.* Guy, *a young musician carrying a saxophone case, enters.*

GUY. Hi, Reb.

REBECCA. You're back early.

GUY. Doesn't feel like that. Feels like I've walked clean through to the soles of my feet.

REBECCA. No luck?

GUY. Luck! You've sure got to have that to get a break in Goli. And I don't get the breaks. *Ja*, what I need is luck, lots of it, like old Sam. Remember him?

REBECCA. He stayed with Lizzie.

GUY. That's him. Old bearded chap. We shared the same room for a time. Old Sam bought his luck . . . small bottles of trash from one of those herbalist quacks in Newclare. Every Friday night he'd trek out there with his pay packet and bring back the latest lucky charm. I argued like hell with him about that stuff. They picked him up just before they started selling the stuff to keep the police away. Poor old Sam. Wish I could believe in it like him.

REBECCA. At the price they charge you've just got to believe.

GUY. Anyway, I couldn't buy it even if I did. I haven't even got enough for a secondhand pair of shoes, and one more session like today and I'll need them.

REBECCA. Patience, Guy, patience. You got the talent.

GUY. Patience! I knocked on the door of every recording shop in town. If I'd known how many chaps were playing the sax I would have stuck to a penny whistle. When my break comes, I won't have enough wind left to blow a false note

REBECCA. Did you try the place Willie mentioned?

GUY. You mean the hotel? That's the nearest I got to a job. They didn't need any musicians... 'But we've got an opening for a kitchen boy.'... 'Opening', mind you! I should have told him, his opening was my back door.

Another bloke gives me a pat on the back after I've blown three bars and says, ever so nicely: 'You boys is just born musicians... born musicians I tell you. You got it in your soul.' So I says: 'But a job, Mister?' And he says: 'Nothing doing. Too many of you boys being born.' You know something, Reb? I should have settled down to book learning. That way you always eat. Like Willie. Now there's a smart Johnny.

REBECCA. Willie's all right.

GUY. All right! He's more than just right, he can't go wrong.

REBECCA. He's just like any other fellow.

GUY. I didn't mean it that way. I know Willie can go wrong, if he does some stupid thing. What I mean is, it's up to himself. But like me now... I know I play well, everyone says so, even some of the top boys. But how does that help me? I still get buggered around. And the way I see it Willie won't make no mistakes. What's this latest thing he's up to?

REBECCA. You mean the course?

GUY. Yes, that's it.

REBECCA. First year B.A. Correspondent.

GUY. There, you see. Now who but Willie would think of that. [*Pause.*] Now... actually... where does that get him?

REBECCA. If he passes, to his second year.

GUY. Well what do you know! [*Pause.*] And then?

REBECCA. The third year.

GUY. Doesn't it end sometime?

REBECCA. If he passes that, he gets his degree. Bachelor of Arts.

GUY. He's a smart one, that Willie. Now tell me, Reb, what does Willie do with his bachelor when he gets him?

REBECCA. [*Laughs.*] A better job... more pay.

GUY. Just like I thought. If there's a catch in it, Willie will find it. You're proud of him, aren't you?

REBECCA. He gave me a better word the other day. I said how we was all proud of him. He corrected me. The word was 'admire'.

GUY. Admire! Proud! What's the difference?

REBECCA. Well, there is a difference. I looked it up in that book of his with all the words. You're proud of something you had a hand in, but you admire someone that went it all alone, Guy. Not even his poor old canary in her rusty cage helped him. Sometimes I wonder if it was best that way.

GUY. You mean you don't think he's doing all right?

REBECCA. No, course not. But it's made him ... independent. A big word, isn't it? But he says it's his ideal and he's getting there. Willie could snap his fingers at anyone ... walk out any time. He just doesn't need anyone. Not you ... not even me.

GUY. When you put that way it does add up. But then remember, Reb, you can't always add up on paper what a man needs, like your instalments on the stove each month. I'm no book bug, but I know that.

REBECCA. Too bad that advice isn't in any of the books he reads.

GUY. He's no fool, Reb. He won't make that mistake.

REBECCA. Let's hope you're right.

GUY. Course I am. Why the two of you's been together for ...

REBECCA. Four years.

GUY. Four years. That's a long time.

[*Pause.*]

REBECCA. You thinking something, Guy?

GUY. Such as?

REBECCA. Like four years, and he hasn't married her yet.

GUY. He's just waiting for his course to finish.

REBECCA. Maybe he is. Anyway, we don't talk much about marrying no more.

GUY. You got nothing to worry about. You and Willie are fine. Just fine.

[*Rebecca exits into the house.* Watson, *who has been seated on the stage since the opening of the scene, is addressed by Guy.*]

GUY. *Ja*, Watson, how's the politics?

WATSON. We're fighting, we're fighting.

GUY. You been fighting for our rights today, Watson?

WATSON. Sort of. Been thinking about my speech for tonight.

GUY. Another meeting?

WATSON. Important one. We've got delegates coming from all the other branches.

GUY. Hey, sounds good. What you going to say?

WATSON. Not sure yet. Round about lunchtime, I had an idea. A stirring call for action! 'The time for sitting still and submitting to every latest injustice is past. We gotta do something about it.' But then I remembered that this was a meeting of the Organizing Committees and they might not like that. Just now, I had another idea. 'We must weld ourselves into a sharp spearhead for the liberatory movement.' That'll have to do.

GUY. You been sitting here the whole day thinking that?

WATSON. The meeting's going to last all night, isn't it?

GUY. Watson, I want to ask you something.

WATSON. Sure, go ahead.

GUY. How do you earn a living?

WATSON. Living? What you mean living?

GUY. You don't get up every morning at six like Willie and old Moses. You don't walk the streets looking for a job like me.

WATSON. I make sacrifices for the cause.

GUY. That must be tough. Telling *us* guys not to work for three pounds a week.

WATSON. You too must make sacrifices for the cause, otherwise the heavy boot of oppression will for ever be on our backs! Hey, that's good. [*He makes a note.*]

GUY. You know something else, Watson, I've never seen you a single day in the streets when there's a riot.

WATSON. We can't all be leaders. Some must lead, some must follow. [*Mrs. Watson calls from offstage in a shrewish voice.*] Coming dear. [*He exits.*]

    [*Rebecca appears at the door shaking a tablecloth.*]

GUY. Say! Do you want to hear something?

REBECCA. Any time.

GUY. I got so fed up this morning I took out the old blowpipe and blew...and what do you know! A wonderful sound comes out. Kind of sad...And this being Friday and every other sucker coming home with a pay packet except me, I've decided to call it 'Friday Night Blues'.

[*Guy plays 'Friday Night Blues'. Willie enters the backyard; he stops and listens to the music.*]

WILLIE. Say, that's all right.

GUY. Friday Night Blues. Inspired by an empty pocket.

WILLIE. No luck?

GUY. Nope. They've picked up all the gold on Eloff Street. No nuggets left for Guy.

WILLIE. Remember what I said. When you're down to the last notch in your belt come along with me. I can always find you something at the office.

GUY. That sounds like a pension scheme. Hold on, man! I haven't even been given a chance yet.

WILLIE. Okay, so your old age is insured.

GUY. That's a comforting thought when you're twenty-two.

REBECCA. Supper will be ready in twenty minutes.

WILLIE. No hurry.

REBECCA. Aren't you hungry?

WILLIE. I'll eat when I see it.

REBECCA. Anything go wrong at work?

WILLIE. Everything is fine, just fine.

REBECCA. I wish you'd tell me, Willie.

WILLIE. Tell you what?

REBECCA. Whatever's bothering you.

WILLIE. Nothing's bothering me. Let's just say I'm a tired man, okay?

REBECCA. Okay. [*She goes into the house.*]

WILLIE [*shouting to her*]. Can you scrape three plates from the pot?

REBECCA [*from inside*]. Who's the extra?

WILLIE. Crazy musician. We'll make him sing for his supper.

GUY. Three cheers for the African Feeding scheme.

WILLIE. You dedicate Friday Night Blues to me, boy.

GUY. It's sad music.

WILLIE. I get sad sometimes.

GUY. Sure, we all do. But this is real sad . . . Sort of . . . you know . . . you got the words.

WILLIE. Melancholy, loneliness, despair. They all add up to the same thing. [*Pause.*] The bus queue was a mile long tonight. That's a lot of people. A mile of sweating shouting bastards, all happy because there was a little bit of gold in their pockets. I've never been so lonely in all my life. It's my song, Guy.

GUY. If you want it, okay. 'To Willie.'

[*He plays 'Friday Night Blues' a second time. In the course of it* Father Higgins *enters, followed by* Tobias, *a newcomer to Johannesburg.*]

HIGGINS. Evening, Willie . . . Guy! We've missed you at the Jazz Club meetings.

GUY. I've been meaning to look in, Father. Just that I've been trying to get started as a professional and that takes time. All of it.

HIGGINS. How far have you got?

GUY. I've reached the first stage. I'm blowing the sax on an empty stomach.

HIGGINS. You'll be all right, Guy. In fact I want to see you about something. Come up to the church on Sunday afternoon and we'll talk about it. How's Willie?

WILLIE. Surprised. It's not often we see you here, Father.

HIGGINS. You should be grateful, it means there is no trouble. You laugh, but it's true. Every time I leave a house here in Sophia Town, I can see the neighbours putting their heads together to discuss the troubles of the family I've just left.

WILLIE. Sophia Town is a fertile acre for troubles, Father.

HIGGINS. Every garden has its weeds, even the white ones.

WILLIE. Yes, I've seen them. I was walking down a street the other day with neat white houses on each side and a well-trained dog snarling at me behind every gate. Those gardens were neat all right, the grass so green I couldn't believe my eyes. And in one of them is a dear old lady with a fork looking for a weed which she finds dying among the flowers, so she digs it out and everything is just fine and blooming nice again. Do you want to plant a daffodil in this yard?

HIGGINS. That's up to you. But I'll tell you what I do want. A little help for a friend. This is Tobias, Tobias Masala. He has just arrived here from the Eastern Transvaal. [*Willie stares at the newcomer with little warmth.*] A simple man, Willie, like so many of our people.

I was wondering if you could help. He'll do anything provided there is enough in it for him to live and maybe save a little each month.

WILLIE. Why do they do it!

HIGGINS. Do what?

WILLIE. That! Why do they come here, like *that*!

HIGGINS. He only wants to live, Willie. You know better than I do the stories they bring with them of sick women and hungry children.

WILLIE. When it rains over here we have to walk up to our ankles throught muck to get into our shacks. There is another patch of muck we have to slosh through every day, the tears and sympathy for our innocent brothers.

HIGGINS. His life is a supreme gift. He must cherish it. He asks for nothing but a chance to do that.

WILLIE. It's muck, I tell you. This is Goli, not a quiet reserve. He wasn't made for this. They flounder, go wrong, and I don't like seeing it.

HIGGINS. Then what was he made for?

WILLIE. His quiet reserve.

HIGGINS. That's what they say about all of us.

WILLIE. I'm no simple Kaffir!

HIGGINS. I'm sorry. I didn't want it to end like this. Come, Tobias, we must go somewhere else.

[*They start to leave.*]

GUY. Come on, Willie, give old Blanker-boy a break.

WILLIE. Don't you understand, Guy, the breaks usually break them.

GUY. He's going to be broken a lot quicker if he's picked up. Have a heart, man! What about that lift job you told me about?

[*Tobias moves up to Willie.*]

TOBIAS. I'm not frightened of work.

GUY. There, you see, old Blanket-boy's got guts.

TOBIAS. At Machadadorp, I work eleven hours when harvest comes.

WILLIE. Why didn't you stay there?

TOBIAS. It's not my district so they say I must go back to my home. But there is no work there and the soil is bad.

GUY. Can you work a lift?

TOBIAS. Lift? Yes, I have lift heavy grain bags on to the lorry.

GUY [*laughing*]. You're all right, Blanket-boy. What do you say, Willie?

WILLIE. I'm making no promises.

HIGGINS. Thanks.

WILLIE. No promises, understand. If he sinks, he sinks.

HIGGINS. Stay here, Tobias. They will try to help you. Good night. [*Exits.*]

TOBIAS. What is it I must lift?

GUY. A building full of white people. Us blacks use the stairs.

TOBIAS. I don't understand.

GUY. That's not important. We're meant to be dumb. What's more important is a little lesson in grammar. Now, what did you call the white induna on the farm where you worked?

TOBIAS. Mr. Higgerty.

GUY. No, Toby. Over here it is '*Baas*'. Do you understand? Just: yes *baas*, no *baas*, please *baas*, thank you *baas*...even when he kicks you on the backside.

   Now take off your hat and grin, come on, cock your head, that's it...and say what I just told you.

TOBIAS. Yes *baas*, no *baas*, please *baas*, thank you *baas*, even when you kick me on the backside.

WILLIE [*jumping forward and striking the hat out of his hands*]. Stop it, damn you!

CURTAIN

SCENE TWO

The backyard about two hours later. It is now dark. The houses are nothing more than shadows, the yellow squares of windows throwing a dim light on the activity in the yard. Attention is focused on a small group of men: Guy, Pinkie, *and* Peter *are playing cards. Watching them is* Tobias, *and seated a little to one side, warming his hands over an open brazier, is old* Moses, *a blind man.* Guy *shuffles a pack of cards.*

128

PINKIE. It's like I said. I'm serving them tea . . . Every eleven o'clock I do it . . . I take it round from the kitchen.

GUY. Pick up your cards.

PETER. Pass.

GUY. Pass.

PINKIE. Now this chap . . .

GUY. What are you doing?

PINKIE. I was telling you, serving the tea. I'm the tea boy in the office.

GUY. The game, Pinkie, the game. Peter passes, I pass. What do you do?

PINKIE. I'll take two. [*He throws out two cards and Guy deals him another two.*]

GUY. Three aces.

PETER. I'm out.

PINKIE. Same here. [*They all throw in their cards. Guy picks them up and shuffles the pack.*]

Now this chap . . . van Rensburg . . . he says he gave me the coupons for his tea, but I haven't got them! And I tell him, I tell him nicely. He starts swearing at me . . . What he doesn't call me!

[*Guy starts dealing.*]

Every door opens, everybody sticks out their head to see who's started the riot and there I am with the tea tray and this chap shouting at me. What would you have done, Guy?

GUY. Pick up your cards.

PINKIE. But he didn't give me a coupon.

GUY. I'll take two.

PETER. Three.

PINKIE. Then the big boss . . . Mr. Cornell . . . he calls me in.

GUY. What are you doing?

PINKIE. Pass. This van Rensburg chap goes in first and has his say. Then I go in. But do I get a chance? You listening, Guy?

GUY. Sure . . . Two pairs.

PETER. Full house.

GUY. What you got?

PINKIE. One pair.

[*Cards are thrown in again. Guy shuffles.*]

PINKIE. So you see, I'm not even given a chance to tell my side of the story. Short and sweet: Cornell says I must apologize by twelve tomorrow morning or I'm sacked. Not even fired, mind you, but sacked! Now what do I do?

GUY. Pick up your cards.

PINKIE. To hell with the cards. I'm asking you for advice and you haven't heard a word I've said.

GUY. I've heard everything you said.

PINKIE. Then what would you do?

GUY. How much do you like your job?

PINKIE. But I tell you he never gave me the coupons for the tea.

GUY. You go and tell that to Watson. He's been sitting here the whole day looking for something to say tonight. Go ask him to raise it in parliament.

PINKIE. You think that's funny?

GUY. You playing or aren't you?

PINKIE. How can I play when I got my problem. Look, Guy, do or don't I apologize to Mr. van Rensburg? That's my problem see. They want me to apologize for something I never done.

GUY. Okay. If it hurts you so much, don't apologize. Now are you playing or aren't you?

PINKIE. But then I lose my job.

GUY. Let's try black lady.

[*Peter nods his agreement. Guy deals for two.*]

PINKIE. What would you do, Peter?

PETER. It's like Guy said. Find what hurts you must: apologizing or losing your job. Then you got your answer.

PINKIE. That sounds nice and easy, doesn't it! Well I don't want to lose my job and I don't want to apologize.

GUY. Sounds like you got to choose one or the other.

PINKIE. But which one, Guy? Which one? What would you do?

GUY. Look, Pinkie . . .

PINKIE. I know . . . But just suppose it was you . . . just suppose. What would you do?

GUY. Well. I suppose it depends.

PINKIE. On what?

GUY. On how you are right now. You sober?

PINKIE. You bet. Smell.

GUY. Well, you're sober, you're calm, you got control of yourself. Now think. It's a good job. It's good pay. It's Friday night. You're going to have yourself a good time. Right?

PINKIE. Right.

GUY. So what! This van Rensburg's not in Sophia Town. You only see him for five minutes every morning and five minutes every afternoon. Why worry about him! Apologize and keep your job.

PINKIE. That makes sense. Guy, you've helped me. That pay packet was welcome, you know, what with Shark coming round. I wouldn't like to be here without five bob when he comes. Of course. It's a job like you said, it's regular pay! That old van Rensburg, we know he was wrong, don't we? So I say: 'I'm sorry, Mr. van Rensburg' and I laugh at him in the kitchen. You're right, Guy!

[*Pinkie makes a move to exit.*]

GUY. Where are you going?

PINKIE. Rosie's. Just a quick one before Shark comes. I'm going to town tonight . . . with something special! Boy, what a woman.

GUY. Go easy on the quickies, Pinkie. Shark doesn't like to be kept waiting.

[*Guy and Peter continue a few hands of black lady. The door of Willie's house opens and he appears in his shirt sleeves.*]

GUY. Reached the end of the alphabet?

WILLIE. Couldn't get started. I begin with the A and the only word I can think of is ass. So I pass it up and go on to B and I get the adjective . . . bloody. Bloody ass! That's what I think of a B.A.

GUY. So? We're all bums in our own way. But stick to your books and you'll be a big one.

WILLIE. What a future! Everybody wants a backside to kick in this country.

GUY [*throwing in his cards*]. I've had enough.

[*To Willie.*] Forget the books tonight if they make you feel so bad.

WILLIE. Forgetting is the problem.

GUY. I always just thought of it as a bad habit.

WILLIE. It is, the way most people do it. What I was getting at was being able to forget just what you wanted to. Learn to do that,

Guy, and you'll be the most contented man in the world. You got
accounts?...Forget them! They summons you?...Forget it?
They jail you?...Forget there's any better place to be.

GUY. I don't know about that.

WILLIE. Take me. Sometimes I forget to put my pen in my pocket
before I go to work. Now how does that help me! But there are
some things you can't forget. They won't allow it. They'd call
that bad memory high treason.

GUY. I don't see that, Willie.

WILLIE. The moment you forget you were black, they'd say you were
red.

MOSES. Willie's right.

GUY. What's this? Another brain specialist.

MOSES. About forgetting. Willie's right.

GUY. Come on, Moses! You been blind so long you just can't
remember nothing no more.

MOSES. Who says? Who says just because my eyes are dark I can't
see nothing? I see things, man. I see things all day long.

GUY. What do you see?

MOSES. My home, my wife, my kiddies. I seen them, man, I tell
you I seen them. Only it's not like you seen things, because with
me they don't change. Like my boy. You know my little boy?
All today when I sat in the sun on the pavement I seen him, *ja*,
I seen him, only I seen him like he was ten years ago. Now he
must be a man.

TOBIAS. How long you been here?

MOSES. A long time.

TOBIAS. When you going home?

MOSES. Home? My boy's coming to fetch me.

TOBIAS. When?

MOSES. He's coming.

WILLIE [*to Guy*]. What's the time?

GUY. Another half an hour to go.

WILLIE [*looking at everybody sitting and waiting*]. He's sure got us
trained, hasn't he?

GUY. As Shark would put it: I've put a lot of money and time into
training you boys. God help the chap that forgets.

WILLIE. I reckon he's about the only one God would want to help.

GUY. If he'd forgotten about Shark the only help God could give would be a free pass into heaven. You'd be finished with the good old earth if you ever forgot eight o'clock on Friday night.

WILLIE. You think we're scared, Guy?

GUY. Sensible. Pay up and you'll at least have the seven days to next Friday.

[*Pinkie reappears. A few drinks have made him slightly more aggressive than when we last saw him.*]

PINKIE. Hey, Guy, how the hell can I apologize!

GUY. You back?

PINKIE. Listen, men, I forgot that argument of yours that convinced me I should apologize. Come on, Guy. How did it go?

GUY. It started with you being sober. You still sober, Pinkie?

PINKIE. I'm not that drunk. I just had a few tots.

GUY. Okay. So now you don't apologize.

PINKIE. I tell you I'm not that drunk. It's a good job. Four pounds a week. For a bachelor man that's good dough. And he says I got to apologize . . . That Cornell . . . he says I got to apologize. Ain't I got rights?

GUY. Go ask Watson.

PINKIE. Come on, Guy. On the level. What would you do? But remember he didn't give you a coupon for a cup of tea. He swore at you for bugger-all.

GUY. Oh shut up! I also got squeals. I been looking for a job for three weeks. Just let each of us keep his squeals to himself.

PINKIE. Well, when you get a job, I hope they tell you to apologize for something you never did. For something you never did.

GUY. My consolation is that by then you'll either be fired or you'll still be working, and I can go to you for advice.

PINKIE. As if I'll give it. You wait. Because it's a problem, you understand, a problem.

[*At this point Pinkie notices Tobias who has been listening carefully to everything said.*] You been listening carefully, I seen you. You're not like these bums.

TOBIAS. I been listening.

PINKIE. Yes, I seen you. Now what would you do? Wait! Before you speak. He never gave you the coupon for the tea. He never

133

did. Because in every office they give you the coupon for the tea
and you put them next to the saucer with the biscuits, and *then*
you give them the tea. But there was no coupon there! He never
gave it to you. So you see he swore at you for bugger-all and
they're asking you to apologize for something you never did. Now
tell me, what would you do?

TOBIAS. I ... [*Pauses, not knowing what to say.*]

PINKIE [*encouraging him*]. *Ja*, come on.

TOBIAS. I don't know.

PINKIE. You don't know. You don't know. Let me go ask Rosie.

GUY [*slapping Pinkie on the back as he passes*]. Cheer up, Pinkie. Go
ask old van Rensburg for his advice. That man takes too much.
[*Pinkie exits.*]

WILLIE. I don't blame him.

TOBIAS [*to Guy*]. You help me with my letter now.

GUY. Is it gonna be long or short?

TOBIAS. Just to my wife, to let her know I have arrived safely in
Johannesburg.

GUY. Okay, but let's be quick. Shark doesn't like to be kept waiting
and I'm on his list. You help me with the spelling, Willie.

WILLIE. Sure.

TOBIAS. Who is this man Shark?

GUY. Insurance. He insures your pay packet. Every Friday night
five bob and you get home safely.
   [*Guy and Tobias exit. Rebecca, who has appeared on stage a few
   minutes earlier, moves up to Willie.*]

REBECCA. Couldn't you get started at all?

WILLIE. Start what?

REBECCA. With the books.

WILLIE. Maybe later. You heard Guy, we're well trained in this
yard. Life starts after eight o'clock.

REBECCA. He always comes on time.

WILLIE. Yes, I suppose we could call that one of his virtues.

   [*Guy's head appears at the window. He calls out 'Maxulu'. Willie
   spells it out.*]

REBECCA. It's true what Guy said.

WILLIE. What did he say?

REBECCA. If you stick to your books you'll go places.

WILLIE. That's a sharp observation.

REBECCA. Why do you get sore every time someone just mentions it?

WILLIE. I'm sick of hearing it.

[*Guy's head appears.*]

GUY. I've got a big one, Willie. 'Circumstances'.

WILLIE [*spelling*]. C-I-R-C-U-M-S-T-A-N-C-E-S.

[*To Rebecca.*] Sick of hearing it. Can you understand that?

REBECCA. No.

WILLIE. I'm sick of being bright when I know it means nothing. I'm sick of going places when I know there is no place to go.

REBECCA. That wasn't what you used to say. When you first got the papers for the course you said it would mean a lot. Extra pay, a better position.

WILLIE [*impatiently*]. Oh . . .

REBECCA. Well, didn't you?

WILLIE. Yes, I said that, two years ago.

REBECCA. Well, isn't it true?

WILLIE. Yes, it's true.

REBECCA. Then why complain?

WILLIE. Complain. I'm not complaining. And if I was, what's wrong with it, when everybody expects me to parcel up my life in the application form for a correspondence course?

[*Guy's head appears at the window. This time the word is 'frustrated'. Willie spells it out.*]

It's just possible that a man can get to thinking about other things than extra pay and a better position.

REBECCA. Such as?

WILLIE. Such as himself. What's he doing? Where does he fit in?

[*Rebecca turns away and walks dejectedly back to the house.*]

I'm sorry, Reb. There's nothing I can do about it. When a man gets to thinking like that he doesn't stop until he finds what he's looking for. Like I told Guy: it's one of those things you can't forget. If I could, life would be simple again. But you've got to know where you're going. I'm doubting what I used to believe in. The shine has worn off. Life feels like an old pair of shoes that everyone is trying to force me into with me knowing I couldn't walk a block in them.

[*Guy's head appears at the window.*]

GUY. Last one. 'Yours faithfully'. One word or two words?

WILLIE. Two words.

REBECCA. Does a man always find the thing he looks for?

WILLIE. If he doesn't he might as well be dead.

REBECCA. I'm going to tidy up. Shall I leave your books out?

WILLIE. Yes, I'll try again.

[*Rebecca exits. Guy and Tobias enter.*]

GUY. How's this for a letter? Toby provided the ideas and I gave
the English. Go on, read it to him, Toby. Show Willie he isn'
the only bum around here with a bit of learning.

TOBIAS [*reading*]. 'Dear Maxulu, I have arrive at Jo'burg. You do no
know it. You cannot see it in your mind. They have building
here like ten mission churches on top of one another, so high you
cannot see the cross on the top. They make mountains by digging
the gold and they tell me they dig the gold under the ground
like moles. You do not know it, Maxulu, it is not like anything
you know. I have not seen one cow, one goat, or even one chicken
but the motor cars are more in one street than the cows of the
chief, and the people more than the biggest impi.

'Here also I find Sophia Town where I stay with Mr. Gu
Modise. I meet his friend, Mr. Willie Seopelo, who will get me
job in one of the tall buildings, taking the whiteman to the top
They call it a lift. But I don't lift, I just press a knob and then
the box takes us all to the top.

'If everything goes right I will send some money this month
call in at the Post Office and buy another blanket. The red ones
If circumstances permit, I will get home on leave in a year. Wa
for me. Get Mr. Mabuza to write to me about you, the children
and the cow. Also get him to read this letter to you. Your
faithfully, your husband. Tobias Masala.'

It's a good letter.

WILLIE. Yeah, it's fine.

TOBIAS [*pointing at Guy*]. He's clever. He writes. But there are thing
I do not say. If she was here, she would feel it in me tonight whe
we lie together, and she would know. But for this letter I nee
words and a word is only a wind. If I must find a wind for th
that I cannot speak, it would be long and soft like that whic

chases the shadows in the grass in summer when we wait for rain. Do you know? The grass is long, the oxen fat, the sun heavy. I remember. I took the oxen into the hills when I was small and I heard that wind and all I could say was, God is lonely. It spoke the thing for which I have no words. The words, Maxulu, the words. You must know when you read that I have not got the words.

WILLIE [*getting up quickly and moving to Guy*]. Did you tell him old Moses has been writing those letters home for ten years?

GUY. Have a heart. Old Moses is fifty. No one finds work at that age. What's the point in discouraging him?

WILLIE. I wasn't thinking of discouragement. Just the truth.

GUY. The truth is Toby is not old, and you're going to help him get a job, and Toby will go back in a year.

WILLIE. A year in this place is like a stray bitch, it drops a litter of ten like itself before it moves on.

GUY. What are you trying to do, Willie?

WILLIE. Stop him dreaming.

GUY. Suppose he is. What's wrong with that? Don't you dream?

WILLIE. I woke up a long time ago.

GUY. I don't get it, Willie. You used to be the one sucker who always had time for a sad story. Any bum could come here and knock on your door and Willie would help.

WILLIE. Have you been talking to Rebecca?

GUY. How does she come into it?

WILLIE. She also found a better past, a better Willie that used to be.

GUY. Okay, let's drop it. When you start getting suspicious about me talking to you like I always talk to you, it's time to shut up.

[*Pinkie, this time quite drunk, appears on stage.*]

PINKIE. He's a bastard. That's what he is! A bloody Dutch bastard. Him and the boss, Mr. Cornell. I bet his mother was also a van Rensburg. Well if they think I'm going to apologize they got another guess coming. Because I got rights. They'll protect me.

GUY. Who?

PINKIE. They.

GUY. Who is they?

PINKIE. Them.

GUY. So you found your solution to the problem.

PINKIE. Solution? It's rights! And I got them. And I don't apologize
because I didn't do nothing. I mean anything. I didn't do something! Anyway, he swore at me for bugger-all and I don't apologize.

[*At this point, Watson, smartly dressed and carrying a briefcase,
appears on his way to a meeting.*]

GUY. Hey Pinkie, there goes Watson. Go and ask him to help you.

PINKIE. Watson, a word with you, my friend. Watson, I know you
can help me because you fight for our rights.

WATSON. Try my best, but I'm in a bit of a hurry, old man.

PINKIE. Wait, Watson, wait. The question is to apologize or not to
apologize.

WATSON. *Ja*, it's a problem all right. I'll think about it.

PINKIE. No, Watson, no! Whatever you do don't think about it.
Because it's life and death to me.

WATSON. Well, you see I'm in a bit of a hurry. There's a meeting
over at Freedom Square and I got to address the delegates.

[*Pinkie and Watson who have moved across the stage now find
themselves suddenly confronted by* Shark *and two of his thugs. Watson
tips his hat and disappears. Pinkie drops back frightened to the other
men who have all stood up and are clustered together.*]

SHARK. Well, isn't anyone glad to see me?

HARRY. Lot of dumb bastards. Come on, *betaal jong!*

SHARK. Don't be so vulgar, Harry. You're always thinking about
money.

HARRY. That's what we come for.

SHARK. Yes, that is true. It is Friday night. All you boys got paid?

HARRY. They wouldn't be here if they wasn't.

WILLIE. Here's your five shillings, Shark. Take it and go.

SHARK. Don't rush me, Willie. You're as vulgar about money as
Harry.

I want to report to you chaps. After all you are entitled to something for your subscription. That is, other than the protection we
give you. Now you boys have been paying very well and very
regular. I reckon this about the best yard in Sophia Town. Isn't
that so, Harry?

HARRY. The very best. We've had no trouble from these bums.

SHARK. And for that reason you've had no trouble from us. You
travel home safely with your pay packets every Friday night. M

boys are all along the way keeping an eye on you chaps. Nobody, but nobody, elbows their way into your hard-earned cash. You know something, I reckon you boys got yourselves a bargain. Now some of my customers haven't been as appreciative as you boys. Yes, in fact I've had quite a bit of trouble. Especially down in Gold Street. Heard about Charlie? Poor Charlie. Tell them about Charlie, Harry.

HARRY. He didn't get off the train tonight.

HARK. That is, not until they found him. Then they carried him off. Looks like foul play. The police are investigating. But hell, what can they do? I mean, those trains are so crowded. It's a shame. They should give you boys a better service, really they should. Okay, Harry, collect.

[*Harry and the other thug move forward collecting from the men. The second thug has a bit of trouble with Tobias who doesn't know what's going on. Harry moves over.*]

HARRY. What are you waiting for?

TOBIAS. I'm waiting for nothing.

HARRY. Then give it.

TOBIAS. Give what?

HARRY. *Vyf* bob, five shillings. *Betaal jong!*

GUY. Lay off him. He's just come here.

HARK. What's the trouble, Harry?

HARRY. Another Charlie, here among the good boys.

GUY. Hang on, Shark, this bloke's a stranger.

HARK. A new arrival! They're always a bit of a risk.

WILLIE. He knows nothing about what's going on. Leave him alone.

HARK. That's stupid advice coming from you, Willie. I mean you got some brains. Aren't you a B.A., boy? A man works hard to get a little business organized, you know, regular customers, and then along comes the stranger who doesn't want to buy. It's a bad example. Who knows, you might be the first one to follow his example.

WILLIE. You've got a monopoly. We all buy what you sell.

HARK. Even the stranger. [*To Tobias.*] Will you buy what I sell?

TOBIAS. What do you sell?

HARK. What do I sell? Protection! This is a bad place.

TOBIAS. [*Bursts into laughter.*] Protection. I'm not a baby.

    [*The atmosphere is suddenly tense. The other men realize Tobias is in trouble.*]

SHARK. What's your name?

TOBIAS. Tobias. Tobias Masala.

SHARK. Tobias? No, that's no good. We'll call you 'stoopid'! [*There is a pause and then Shark's voice is almost at a scream.*] Stupid! Because that's what you are. A dumb bloody ox. Okay, Harry.

    [*Harry and the other thug move like lightning. A knife flashes, it is quick and sudden. Tobias is left lying on the ground. Shark turns and looks at the men, then spits on the body and leaves. Willie moves forward and bends down to the dead Tobias. He withdraws instantly, rubbing the palms of his hands on his trousers.*]

CURTAIN

SCENE THREE

Willie's room. It is Sunday night. He is sitting at a table with a number of books open in front of him, but he is not giving them any attention. Behind him Rebecca is cleaning up after the evening meal.

REBECCA. Oh yes, and something else. Betty and Solly is engaged. They want to get married in November. I met them on the street. He asked about you. Wants to know when you going to visit him. Says I must tell you to leave the books alone one evening and to go over. He's changed his job, you know. In a lawyer's office now, getting much better pay. That's how they can get married. I'll be seeing her tomorrow. Shall I tell her we'll be over sometime this week? Willie!

WILLIE. Sorry. What's that you were saying?

REBECCA. Am I disturbing you?

WILLIE. No, I wasn't reading.

REBECCA. You wasn't listening either.

WILLIE. Just tired, I guess.

REBECCA. Been at it all afternoon.

WILLIE. At what?

REBECCA. Books, silly. You been learning all afternoon.

WILLIE. Yes . . . yes, that's it. I been learning all afternoon.

REBECCA. Then give it a rest now. What you been doing? History?

WILLIE. You don't have to talk about it as if you were interested.

REBECCA. But I am.

WILLIE. All right. You are.

REBECCA. Why always so suspicious? Every time I try to understand you shut up, like you didn't want to share anything.

WILLIE. I share the money. [*Pause.*] I'm sorry. I didn't mean to say it.

REBECCA. You just got so many chances of saying a thing like that.

WILLIE. I didn't mean it.

REBECCA. Then why did you say it?

WILLIE. I don't know.

REBECCA. Maybe it's because you want to use up all your chances.

WILLIE. What are you getting at?

REBECCA. That although I don't read as much as you I can understand simple language, so if you want to say 'get out' say it and I'll go.

WILLIE. What does that mean?

REBECCA. We aren't married.

WILLIE. So?

REBECCA. So there's nothing to stop you from saying it. But remember when you say it, that I'm not in here for the money.

WILLIE. I don't want to say it, Reb.

REBECCA. Then stop acting like you wanted to. I can't help it if it looks that way to me, Willie. I haven't changed, I'm the same Rebecca. But you aren't like you used to be. We don't talk about things any more.

WILLIE. Like getting married.

REBECCA. Yes, that's one of them. Why don't we, Willie? I mean talk, even just talk.

WILLIE. Maybe because you don't talk about that sort of thing in a voice as rusty as old junk in a backyard.

REBECCA. Can't we change that?

WILLIE. Change what? My voice? Must I only start cooing like a turtle-dove in the blue gum to have everything back cosy and warm again?

REBECCA. What's wrong with having life cosy and warm?

WILLIE. Nothing, absolutely nothing if you're still up there in the blue gum. But something has shaken it and I've fallen out of the nest. It's not cosy and warm down here and I don't see how can kid myself that it is.

REBECCA. Okay, Willie. You've said that so many different ways can't count them no more. But please, just for once, try and tel me what's shaken you down.

WILLIE. 'A slow soft wind of loneliness.' That doesn't mean much to you, does it?

REBECCA. Not a thing. You couldn't have been very settled in you nest if a slow soft wind kicks you out.

WILLIE. I was a fool to have said it. I should have known yo wouldn't understand.

REBECCA. Understand? When all you give me is something about wind that doesn't mean a thing to me. Try it simple, Willie Have you grown sick of me? Just say yes and I'll understand.

WILLIE. I'm sick of my whole life. Everything! Every single thin that I've done or believed in looks stupid. Is that clear enoug for you?

[*A knock on the door. Guy's voice calls 'Anybody home?'*]

REBECCA [*pulling herself together*]. Coming, Guy. [*She opens the door*

GUY [*entering*]. Willie at home? There you are. Where were you thi afternoon? I knocked twice and got no answer.

[*Pause.*]

REBECCA. I thought you stayed home this afternoon.

GUY. Hey? Have I said anything I shouldn't?

WILLIE. It's okay, Guy. [*There is another pause. Willie can fe Rebecca's eyes on him.*] I went for a walk.

REBECCA. Guy says he knocked twice.

GUY [*quick to make amends*]. Yes, but they was very close togethe I knocked on the door, went over to Moses to ask if he'd see Willie, then I came straight back and knocked a second tim thinking maybe Willie was sleeping. Honest, Reb.

WILLIE. I went for a walk.

142

GUY [*breaking the uneasy silence*]. Tell you what I wanted to see you about. The big show they're putting on for the mission ... know about it? Top-line talent. Well, one of the boys ... plays the sax ... has fallen ill and I take his place. I get paid. [*Guy looks excitedly from Willie to Rebecca. The excitement in his eyes fades at their poor response.*] I just thought you might like to know.

WILLIE. It's a good break.

GUY [*recovering*]. You think so? You really think so?

WILLIE. Of course, it's a big show. You'll be heard by the right people.

GUY. That's what I thought. But I haven't told you the best yet. I play a solo and you know what its going to be? 'Friday Night Blues'! How's that? I'm going to keep it just like I told you. 'Inspired by an empty pocket.' You'll be along, won't you, to hear I mean? Being a soloist, I get my two seats and want you and Reb to have them. And I'll see they're front row. Nothing but the best.

REBECCA. Thanks, Guy.

GUY. I couldn't have done a thing without you and Willie.

REBECCA. Had any supper?

GUY. See what I mean?

REBECCA. There's coffee, bread and jam.

GUY. I was so excited, I've forgotten to eat.

REBECCA. Now's as good a time as any.

GUY. Let me buy something. I still got a few bob. Shark didn't take it all ... [*His sentence trails off into silence.*]

WILLIE. That's all right. I think we have all nearly forgotten by now.

GUY. I reckon so. A fellow gets all excited about something that has happened to him, and you forget about other things. [*Pause.*] They buried him this afternoon.

WILLIE. Did they?

GUY. Why you always so tough about old Blanket-boy, Willie?

WILLIE. Do you think a few tears can help him now?

GUY. Toby was all right, Willie. There's a lot of those chaps about. They don't mean nothing wrong. It's like Father Higgins said, he just wanted to work.

WILLIE. And it all turned out like I told Father Higgins ... They come to the city and go wrong.

GUY. But Toby didn't go wrong.

WILLIE. What's right about being six feet underground!

GUY. I see what you mean. Yes, there's nothing right about that. I thought you meant wrong . . . like Shark . . . You know. Toby didn't have enough savvy to peddle dagga. He was a good chap. When we was writing that letter in my room on Friday night he told me about himself. What he was going to do with his cash when he got home.

WILLIE. Let's leave that for somebody who wants to write a sad story about a black skin.

GUY [*placating*]. Sure . . . sure.

[*There is a knock at the door. Rebecca opens it. Father Higgins stands there holding a bundle.*]

HIGGINS. Hello, Rebecca. Is Willie home?

REBECCA. Yes, come in.

HIGGINS [*entering*]. Hello, Willie, Guy.

GUY. I'm sorry I didn't get to the funeral this afternoon, Father but I was jumping around getting organized for the concert.

HIGGINS. I understand. Actually it went off all right, didn't it, Willie

GUY. Willie!

REBECCA. Willie?

HIGGINS. Yes, Willie was there. Just the two of us and the diggers.

WILLIE. What do you want, Father?

HIGGINS. Am I disturbing you?

WILLIE. Yes.

HIGGINS. It's about Tobias. There will have to be a letter home t his people and this death certificate.

GUY. There is also a few of his things in my room. Shall I g them for you, Father?

HIGGINS. Please. I'll make up a parcel and send it all back.

GUY. Won't be a minute. [*Exit.*]

REBECCA. Sit down, Father. Can I give you some coffee?

HIGGINS. Don't go to any trouble.

REBECCA. No trouble. It's ready.

HIGGINS. How are you keeping?

REBECCA. So so.

HIGGINS. So so? Why are Sundays always so miserable in Sophia Town?

WILLIE. Nothing to do except sit around and think. And what we got to think about ain't so good either.

HIGGINS. The Lord's Day.

WILLIE. You aren't shouting Hallelujah any louder than us.

HIGGINS. How can I, Willie? You were at the graveside with me.

WILLIE. What was it you wanted to see me about?

HIGGINS. A letter home to Tobias's family. I only knew him from the few minutes he spent with me when he came for help. I was thinking that someone over here, maybe you, got to know him a little better and . . .

WILLIE. And you want me to write the letter.

HIGGINS. Yes. I meant to speak to you about it this afternoon.

WILLIE. I can't very well say no.

HIGGINS. I don't want to force you. Don't force yourself.

WILLIE. I'll write it. Let's leave it at that.

HIGGINS. [*Takes up the bundle of clothing he brought in with him. He feels around in it and finds the letter Guy wrote for Tobias.*] I suppose the address will be the same as on this. Do you think this letter should go with it?

WILLIE. No.

HIGGINS. It was his last letter home.

WILLIE. It's better they don't get it.

HIGGINS. Why?

WILLIE. Because it's full of dreams. Because it tells them what a wonderful place Johannesburg is and asks them to wait for him. If that letter goes I don't write.

HIGGINS. I leave it to you.

[*Guy appears. He has a few of Tobias's belongings with him.*]

GUY. This was all there was.

HIGGINS. I'll parcel it up with the rest. Not very much, is it?

GUY. There's a little money here. [*He counts.*] Five shillings.

[*Willie and Guy exchange a look. Higgins sees it.*]

HIGGINS. Five shillings. I've heard about that.

WILLIE. So have we.

HIGGINS. Yes, you must know a lot.

WILLIE. Over here you only know as much as is good for you.

HIGGINS. Even someone like yourself?

WILLIE. Why should I be different from the rest?

HIGGINS. I just thought you might be.

WILLIE. Say it straight.

HIGGINS. All right. Tobias was an innocent man. A simple and a good man. He came to me on Friday looking for a chance to work and live. He asked for nothing more. This afternoon, two days later, I buried him. You know what it was like. You stood at the graveside with me. A fistful of flowers and a wooden cross. I buried others like that, Willie. It wasn't my first time even if it might have been yours. I know life is 'cheap' here; I've heard that sort of talk until I'm sick of it. But something inside me finds five shillings just a little too cheap. I was hoping you might have felt the same.

WILLIE. Nobody over here thinks five shillings expensive!

HIGGINS. Then why does it keep on happening? There are going to be others like Tobias. They'll walk in full of hope and be carried out in a coffin.

GUY. So?

HIGGINS. It doesn't have to be like that if only someone will do something about it.

GUY. Such as?

HIGGINS. Someone must have seen what happened out there on Friday night. Go along to the police and give a sworn statement. Get others to do the same. If only we can get as far as an official charge...

GUY. Whew! You're not asking for courage... you're asking for suicide. This character we're up against, he doesn't go to church. Maybe you don't know him like we do.

HIGGINS. Ask for police protection.

GUY. Don't you understand? He's got shares in the police station. If I go along like you said, they'd let me talk for fifteen minutes. Sure, they'd listen to all I said. But when I was finished: 'Where's your pass?' Now I haven't got a permit to stay in Sophia Town, so I'd be in for fourteen days. And when I come out...? If you think Toby was cheap at five bob I wouldn't be able to sell myself for a sixpence. He'd be waiting and he'd get me. You can forget

about the police. They protect a fellow like Shark. You see they're
only interested in our passes. But a Kaffir laying a charge against
a criminal . . . that would be a joke. We are all criminals. Look,
Father, don't be hard on us. You know what I've just said better
than any other white.

HIGGINS. Sure. I'll leave this letter with you, Willie. Thanks for the
coffee, Rebecca. Good night.

GUY. Say, Father, is it still all right for the show?

HIGGINS. Of course, Guy. Practice hard.

[*He leaves with the bundle of Tobias's clothing. There is a pause
after his exit. Guy and Rebecca look at Willie.*]

REBECCA. Why didn't you tell us you went to the funeral?

WILLIE. Why should I? Everybody has just about forgotten what
happened on Friday night.

GUY. But not you.

WILLIE. Give me time, give me time.

GUY. It's your advice, Willie. If you can forget, life will be easier.
Remember saying that, on Friday night?

WILLIE. I remember.

GUY. Those were true words. I mean . . . if you can't forget you
might . . .

WILLIE. What?

GUY. I don't know. That's why I say, try hard, Willie. Try real hard.

WILLIE. I said give me time, didn't I?

GUY. Sure.

WILLIE. What's eating you, Guy? Speak up.

GUY. You don't look as if it's going too easy.

WILLIE. Should it be easy? What are we saying? Easy! We make a
proud job of living, don't we. Let's make it easy. Let's make the
whole thing easy. Easy come, easy go.

GUY. That's the way it is.

WILLIE. I know the way it is! Only it's not quite so easy to take
at times.

GUY. Life's hard enough for a bloke to want to soften it up a little.

WILLIE. The only way we can soften life is by softening ourselves.

GUY. Like how?

WILLIE. Like forgetting a silly bastard was killed out there and we stood around because that way life was easy.

GUY. Hey Willie! Look...look at me. You know me, Guy, the bum you always help. You owe me nothing, Willie, so what I say is on the level, see. Willie. Forget it. Go back to your books, grab yourself a hunk of living, get married...Do anything you like, but forget Friday night.

WILLIE. We make a proud job of living.

GUY. Do you want to end up dead?

WILLIE. How else does a man hope to end up?

GUY. Okay, you're quick on the words. But how about next Friday... next Friday...like Tobias out there in the yard.

WILLIE. Will you forget that just as easily?

REBECCA. Willie! What are you saying! You want to chase the whole world away from you? Guy speaks to you like a friend and what does he get? A kick in the backside.

WILLIE. I'm sorry, Guy.

GUY. Skip it. Father Higgins made us all jumpy talking like that about doing something.

WILLIE. Guess so. That and the funeral. It's still close, you know, this afternoon. And now this letter he's asked me to write back to the woman. Let me get this off my chest and I'll feel better. The whole business is hanging round my neck. Yes, that's it. Let me get this off and I'll feel better.

GUY. Of course. You'll write a good letter. Nobody could ask for more.

[*Willie sits at the table and takes up a pen and starts writing.*]

WILLIE. 'Dear Mrs. Masala...' [*The words dry up. He tears off the paper and tries again.*] 'Dear Mrs. Masala...Dear Mrs. Masala.' [*Again the words dry up. Willie looks up and sees Guy and Rebecca watching him.*]

CURTAIN

SCENE FOUR

*The setting is the same as the last scene. It is Friday night, five days
later. The time is about seven o'clock in the evening. Rebecca is alone
in the room, and is hurriedly packing a suitcase. She is obviously
upset and having a hard time controlling her emotions. There is a
knock at the door. She starts, looks around quickly for some place to
hide he suitcase. The knock comes a second time and she calls out ...*

REBECCA. Who's there?

GUY [*from outside*]. Only me. Open up.
  [*Rebecca opens the door and Guy comes in. He is breathless and
  looks quickly round the room.*]

GUY. Where is he?

REBECCA. I don't know.

GUY. What's he doing, Reb? Tell me. What does Willie think he's
  doing?

REBECCA. I don't know.

GUY. He's asking for trouble like I've never seen any man ask for
  it and that's for sure. That's for damned sure. They're talking
  about it on every street corner. Willie Seopelo ... Willie Seopelo ...
  If Shark hasn't heard about it by now he must be stone deaf.
  Aren't you worried?

REBECCA. Worried?

GUY. Yes, worried. You know he went to the police station.

REBECCA. Did he?

GUY. Cut it out, Reb, this is no joke. The police station! To report
  Shark! And they laughed at him just like I said they would, and
  now everybody in Sophia Town knows he went. And that includes
  Shark. Willie's making it dangerous just to be a friend of his.
  Listen, Reb, do you realize what this means?

REBECCA. Well what do you want me to do?

GUY. Look worried, get scared. Because it's Willie.

REBECCA. It's always Willie.

GUY. Well this time it's for sure. Didn't you try to stop him?

REBECCA. Have you ever tried arguing with Willie? ... When you
  don't even know half the words for the things you want to say?

GUY. Then why's he doing it, Reb? There must be a reason. [*Pause.*]

Didn't you ask him?

REBECCA. I did. He said he wanted to be able to sleep at night.

GUY. That's all?

REBECCA. That's all he said.

GUY. Is he coming back here?

REBECCA. I suppose so.

GUY. Suppose? Look, what's going on here? Don't you know what Willie does any more?

REBECCA. He doesn't tell me and I stopped asking.

GUY. What's happening to the world!

REBECCA. You been away too long, Guy. You got a lot to catch up on.

GUY. Only four days...I had to do my practising for tonight in town. It's only four *days!* Things can't change as much as this in four days. Anyway I came as soon as I heard about it. Pinkie came round and told me about it this afternoon. But why, Reb, what's got into him?

REBECCA. Stop asking me like that.

GUY. Then who must I ask?

REBECCA. I don't know, but don't ask me because I don't know and I don't care.

GUY. Don't care!

REBECCA. That's what I said. I don't care.

GUY. Hey easy Reb, easy. You don't mean that.

REBECCA. Why shouldn't I mean it? I'll say it again: I don't care. I mean every word of it.

GUY. That means you not going to put a bunch of flowers on Willie's grave on Sunday. Yes! On his grave. Because if you think it's going to be any other way you're wrong. He hasn't got a snowball's chance in hell against Shark. And if you don't care about it all right. What you doing, Reb? What's this?

REBECCA. A suitcase and I'm packing it.

GUY. You're getting out?

REBECCA. Can you give me a good reason for staying?

GUY. Yes. Willie. Look Reb, let me explain very clearly: if we don't do something he's finished. Everybody's waiting to see what happens. Shark knows that. He knows that if he doesn't put Willie down hard, he might as well pack up and try his hand at a *dagga* racket. So he's going to put Willie down hard. We've got to stop that.

REBECCA. How are you going to stop it?

GUY. I'll speak to Willie.

REBECCA. What are you going to say that I haven't already said? Tell me, Guy, what are you going to find in your friendship that I couldn't find in my love?

GUY. It can't be as bad as that.

REBECCA. Tell me what you're going to say to him.

GUY. It can't be like you said, Reb.

REBECCA. Why can't it?

GUY. Because Willie is sensible. He listens to reason.

REBECCA. You can't reason with a mad man. You think I'm talking wild now, carried away by my emotions as Willie always said. Well this time it isn't true. I've been carried away nowhere. For four days I've lived in here with Willie and watched him change until I don't recognize him anymore. I've sat here and watched Willie's big brain get hold of him and destroy him. He sat here day and night for four days with one idea until it nearly drove me mad as well . . . until it drove him to the police station.

GUY. What was this idea, Reb?

REBECCA. Tobias!

GUY. Toby. I should have known.

REBECCA. But don't think he told me. Not Willie. Not any more. I could be the doormat he wipes his feet on for all the notice he takes of me.

[*She dips her hand into a wastepaper basket and pulls out a handful of crumpled papers.*]

Do you see this? It's the letter Father Higgins asked him to write to Tobias's wife. Well that's all he does . . . and he can't even do it. Look at this. Do you see? Our address and then 'Dear Mrs. Masala.' He never gets any further.

GUY. But Willie was so damned good at letters.

REBECCA. This one he can't write. He's been sitting with this letter ever since last Sunday.

GUY. So he couldn't forget. But why? Have you tried speaking to Willie, Reb? I mean really tried.

REBECCA. Oh, Guy! What you think I been doing here these four

151

days? What? Do you think I just been sitting here watching... making coffee when he wanted it... cooking his food. I knowed with something inside me that this was our last chance, and if you think I've wasted it I'd call God down to give witness. If he even heard half my prayers he would have a lot to say. I've tried everything—everything a woman can try I've tried in here. I've tried just being with him, just being here so that if he wanted something he could ask. I've tried it on that bed at night... offered him the comfort only a woman can offer a man. I would have let him take me like a dog takes a bitch in the street if I thought it would be comfort. Because I know that if I could have given Willie that, in any way, there would still be hope. [*Pause.*] I haven't been able to comfort, help or do anything a woman should for her man.

GUY. And now you're clearing out?

REBECCA. Clearing out or being kicked out. I don't know which it is. I only know that I'm going, that I should have been gone a long time ago. I've overstayed my time.

GUY. There is no time to you and Willie.

REBECCA. Hearing you speak like that makes me realize what Willie must have thought of the things I said. You sound stupid, Guy. It's over and you're still trying to kid yourself it isn't, like I been doing. And all the time Willie knew it was over. Only he was too much of a gentleman to kick me out. He waited for me to realize it was time to go.

GUY. Before you go, Reb... Remember you still love him.

REBECCA. Love him! I feel like I been to bed with one man and woke up to find a stranger beside me. I might have loved the man I went to sleep with, but the man I found this morning fills me with shame. And it's so deep, Guy, I just want to run away from what causes it.

GUY. He needs you, Reb.

REBECCA. He hasn't said it.

GUY. He's blind! He doesn't know what he's up against.

REBECCA. Well, if he doesn't it's no use. Can't you see that, Guy? Willie is a man and because of that you can't force a thing down his throat like a mother with a child that won't take medicine. He's a man, Guy, so he lives his own life and if he doesn't want anything, he doesn't want it and this is how it is with me. It's over You walked in at the end. Life isn't like a gramophone record where you can go back to the beginning.

GUY. Where you going?

REBECCA. Back to my mother.

GUY. That's going to be tough, Reb.

REBECCA. Only place to go. Anyway it's easier than staying here.
[*The door opens and Willie enters.*]

WILLIE. I thought you were practising in town.

GUY. I came as soon as I heard.

WILLIE. About me going to the police?

GUY. Yes. Well, what are you waiting for?

WILLIE. What do you mean?

GUY. You're not going to sit there and wait for him, are you?

WILLIE. You mean Shark.

GUY. Who else is going to visit you?

WILLIE. If he comes . . .

GUY. If he comes! What do you think he's going to do? Run away? You think you've scared him? He's going to be around here as certain as today's Friday, and it won't be a social call.

WILLIE. Do you want me to run away?

GUY. Yes. They're not nice words but that about describes it.

WILLIE. I'm sick of running away.

GUY. You've never run away from anything before, Willie.

WILLIE. I've been running away my whole life.

REBECCA. Willie . . .

WILLIE. Don't try and tell me that's not true because it is.

REBECCA. Listen to me . . .

WILLIE. No! For once there is something I'm going to work out for myself. The way I want it, the way I feel it should be worked out, without advice or kind encouragement from anyone.

GUY. And we must sit around and watch you make a balls-up of everything.

WILLIE. If you can't take it, get out.

GUY. You coming, Reb?

WILLIE. Guy! Guy, please. Turn off the pressure, man. You're pushing me. I've been pushed so much I can't take it any more.

GUY. Who's pushing you?

WILLIE. Everybody.

GUY. Don't let it bother you no more. I've stopped as from right now.

WILLIE. Look, Guy. *I've* got to live my life, not you.

GUY. Why do you think I asked you to clear out? Because I want you to live it, not throw it away.

WILLIE. I'm not throwing it away.

GUY. Okay, okay. Now you tell me what you think Shark is going to do when he comes around here looking for you. Pat you on the back, shake your hand? Sure they might do that before they put the knife into you like with Tobias. Willie ... You remember last Sunday, here in this room. Last Sunday, I said that the man who thought of trying to report Shark to the police wouldn't be worth a sixpence. You remember me saying that? You remember me saying that even if he did get as far as the police station it still wouldn't mean a thing because the police wouldn't be interested. You remember all that, Willie ... You know it, don't you?

WILLIE. Yes.

GUY. You know all that but you went along to the police. Now forget the big words, Willie ... I want you to tell me in short ones that I can understand why you went.

WILLIE. I went for myself. For myself. Not to get Shark. Before I even start reckoning with him I've got myself to think about, the part I played in Tobias's death. The emotion inside me is shame, not anger, shame. You see, Guy, I'm involved as surely as I stood there and watched him go down.

GUY. You had nothing to do with it. None of us did.

WILLIE. Didn't we?

GUY. No.

WILLIE. Then why can't I forget? Why? Why can't I write that letter?

GUY. You was always so good at letters.

WILLIE. Good at letters! How do you speak kindly of a man's death when the only truth about it is its stupidity? How do you tell a woman that her man died for bugger-all and that his death means bugger-all. Where's the comfort, Guy? Where? Go squeeze Tobias's blood out of the mud in the yard before you ask me to find it. Comfort, Guy, not a cliché. Not a stupid 'I'm sorry' or

'He was a good man' but a sweetness as clean as his mother's pain when she dropped him into the world. Tobias is dead, and all I can say is that there is a little more muck in our backyard.

GUY. And I thought you didn't like him.

WILLIE. Of course I didn't. I hated him. I hated him because I feared him. These 'simple men' with their innocence and dreams. How can we dream? When I was a child I used to lay awake at night in the room where my mother and us kids used to sleep. I used to lay awake and think. I'd say to myself, 'You're black.' But hell it was so dark I couldn't see my own hand. I couldn't see my blackness, and I'd get to thinking that maybe the colour wasn't so important after all . . . and because I'd think that I could dream a little. But there was always the next morning with its light and the truth. And the next morning used to come so regularly and make the dream so stupid that I gave up dreaming. Tobias reminded me of too much, Guy. He was going to make some money and live happily ever after. The cosy little dream . . . like this! Willie and Rebecca lived happily ever after! That's how the fairy stories end and it's stupid because out there is life and it's not ending happily.

REBECCA. Don't worry about that no more. You got your unhappy ending.

GUY. Hold it, Reb. Look, Willie, there's nothing wrong with a man trying to make a decent life for himself.

WILLIE. Yes there is, if he uses it as a fire exit every time life gets a little hot.

GUY. So what must everybody do? Chuck up all they got and live in rags?

WILLIE. I'm not talking about everybody. I'm talking about myself. You can do a good thing for a wrong reason . . .

REBECCA. Shut up! I know it all. Every word he's going to say . . . I've heard it all before.

GUY. She's pulling out, Willie.

WILLIE. Leaving?

GUY. That's it. Reb is leaving, Willie. Say something!

REBECCA. So at last I found it, Willie.

WILLIE. What?

REBECCA. I found the thing that leaves you without words. We've

been in here four years . . . I don't think there was anything I done
in those four years for which you didn't have something to say.
Is there really nothing, Willie? Not even 'I don't want you to go.'
What about 'Goodbye'?

[*Rebecca leaves.*]

GUY. You let her go like that? You let Reb walk out like she just come
to sweep the floor? She's at the steps, Willie . . . Run, man . . . run.
Willie, I'm asking you!

WILLIE. I can't.

GUY. Did I see it end . . . here, in front of me? Did I see Reb leave,
and you standing there saying nothing, doing nothing?

[*The door bursts open, Pinkie rushes in.*]

PINKIE. Willie! . . . Shark's outside. He's asking for you.

CURTAIN

SCENE FIVE

*The backyard of Scenes One and Two. The various characters,
Watson, Moses, et al. are standing around tensely, their attention
focused on Shark and his two thugs. The door of Willie's room
opens and he comes out followed by Guy and Pinkie.*

SHARK. Hi, Willie. How's life treating you, boy?

WILLIE. What do you want?

SHARK. What do I want? Did you hear that, Harry?

HARRY. *Ja.* He asked what you want.

SHARK. What do I want?

HARRY. Five bob.

SHARK. There you go again. Always thinking about money. You're
crude, Harry, real crude. I wanted to chat with you, Willie. A
quiet talk just between you and me. This place is crowded, let's
go into your room. Harry will see to the business. Okay, Willie?
I just want to talk, boy.

WILLIE. Say it here if you're man enough. You don't go into my house.

SHARK. Why not?

WILLIE. It's clean.

PINKIE. ... Ah ... ah ... Here's my five shillings, Shark.

SHARK. Go away, little man. Okay, I'll say it here. I was going to spare you the embarrassment, but I'll say it. You done me dirty, Willie. You done me all wrong. You went along to the police like any cheap blabbermouth to cause me trouble. Did you hear that, all of you? To the police ... the bastards who lock us up for not carrying our passes. That's who Willie went to see. You got to watch him. Because if you don't, he'll report you as well. Yes, he will. You, Watson ... he'll report you to the Special Branch. He's ambitious, this boy ... He'll do it. Now Willie, I reckon it's my public duty to tell you, to warn you that it's got to stop. Do you understand? S-T-O-P. I'm telling you, because these men pay me to protect them, and that's what I intend doing. It's your type that takes advantage of them. Like that little man over there ... he's just a little man. What can he do about a type like you? Or Watson. Good old Watson, who fights for our rights and fights so damned well, he hasn't realized how dangerous you are, a government spy ... right under his nose. Now ... I'm prepared to give you a chance ...

WILLIE. Like Tobias.

PINKIE. Take it easy, Willie.

SHARK. What about him?

WILLIE. The 'chance' you gave him.

SHARK. He was getting rough with Harry. It was self-defence. [*To Harry.*] Wasn't it, boy?

WILLIE. It was murder.

SHARK. I could sue you for that. For making incriminating statements against me. I got witnesses. Haven't I, boys? [*Addressing the others.*] I came here ... I just wanted to talk to Willie, but you all heard the way he's been carrying on against me. He's asking for trouble. [*To Willie.*] You're lucky you got me to protect you against yourself.

WILLIE. I might have been.

SHARK. Might?

WILLIE. Past tense. The protection is finished. I don't buy any more.

SHARK. You're not going to pay?

WILLIE. That's what I said.

PINKIE. No, Willie.

SHARK. On my way down here I heard talk like that. Ain't you feeling well, boy? You do look sort of pale. Strange that, huh . . . how pale a black skin can get when the man inside it is shit-scared of dying.

WILLIE. I don't scare that easily.

SHARK. Look boy, you went to the police station. Now that was a silly thing to do. But I can square that up. After all, you might have thought it your duty and I got no objection to a man doing his duty, even though I would have liked you to come and see me about it first. Anyway I can forget your little jaunt to the police station . . . even though I know what you tried to tell them. Yes, I know, Willie. I know everything! But I am willing to forget that. I can square it up with the boys. But I can't forget this talk about not paying. That's insulting. It's revolution! Haven't you bums had enough already?

WILLIE. Are you finished?

SHARK. Look, Willie . . . are you trying to scare me? With what? What you got that can scare me? These bums? Is that it? You going to organize a vigilance committee?

WILLIE. They got nothing to do with this.

SHARK. They'd better not if they know what's good for them.

WILLIE. Is that the lot?

SHARK. The lot! I haven't even started with you yet. And when I do you'll wish you'd stuck to the sample I gave you last Friday night. Listen, Willie, let's talk this over sensible-like. What's worrying you? Old Stoopid? Is that it? Okay. Here's a pound. One pound of the money I've sweated for. Send it to the woman in the kraal. Tell her it comes from a sympathizer. Now how's that?

WILLIE. Go stick that on the nail in your lavatory.

SHARK. If that's the way you want it, okay. Now listen to me. Two hours, Willie . . . two hours. You be here with your five bob waiting in two hours' time, or clear out. Talk big then. Because I'll be coming around for you . . . just for you.

HARRY. Why wait?

SHARK. No, this is business. Serious business ... and I want Willie to think about my proposition. [*He moves off with his thugs. Just before his exit he turns.*] Two hours, Willie!
  [*Shark's exit leaves behind a dead silence.*]

PINKIE. Don't you think you'd better start packing, Willie?

WILLIE. Packing?

PINKIE. *Ja*, He's only given you two hours. Aren't you going, Willie?

GUY. How can you ask Willie such a stupid question, Pinkie? Willie here is going to show us how to live ... how to live really big ... Aren't you, Willie? You are going to show what miserable bums we are and how a man really behaves ... how a man really throws his life away. Ain't I right, Willie? But there's something I've left out. Why don't you say it?

WILLIE. Say what?

GUY. Why don't you ask who's going to keep you company in two hours' time?

PINKIE. Don't talk like that. It makes me nervous.

GUY [*still at Willie*]. Because that's what you're thinking, isn't it?

WILLIE. I'm not thinking anything.

GUY. You bet you aren't, because I've never seen anything so Goddamn stupid in all my life. And you are the clever one, remember, the Thinker!

WILLIE. Am I?

GUY. That's a good question. Maybe I should have said 'was'. Because you been sitting in there the whole week thinking and this is the result. Anyway you'd better start again, start thinking quick because you got a lot to think about ... and only two hours to do it.

PINKIE. Hey Willie, you want to borrow five bob? I got paid today. I can manage it. You want it? Because you see Willie, I got a good job. Four pounds a week that's good dough for a bachelor man, huh? I don't want to lose the job, Willie ... Maybe I should say I don't want the job to lose me.

WILLIE. This doesn't involve you, Pinkie, or anybody else.

PINKIE. I wasn't just thinking of myself.

WILLIE. No?

PINKIE. No ... What I mean is ... we had one killing in here that was all a bad mistake. Let's not have another. Death is kind of infectious, you know. It's like a disease ... it spreads. Look at old

Tobias . . . He went . . . and now you . . . maybe we follow.

WILLIE. Whatever happens you just carry on like nothing had happened. Like we all did last Saturday.

PINKIE. But you don't have to . . . He's given you a chance . . . a chance to live.

WILLIE. What does that make him? God Almighty?

WATSON. Look, maybe I can help. I don't want to get involved in something that doesn't concern me . . . I mean . . . I wasn't here when this . . . this . . .

WILLIE. He called it self-protection.

WATSON. *Ja* . . . when this self-protection happened. But I been a neighbour of all of you for a long time . . . and . . . What I'm trying to say is . . . ah . . . What can these chaps do against a man like Shark?

WILLIE. I told you before that's their problem and I'm not trying solve it, for anybody.

WATSON. Now that's just where I think I can clear up the whole business. I'm prepared to put forward a resolution at the next congress, deploring the high incidence of crime and calling for an immediate . . .

PINKIE. Watson, why don't you go home? But he's right, Willie. What can we do about Shark?

WILLIE. Let's get one thing straight. I haven't been having nightmares about what we can do or what we can't. I been waking up at night sweating with shame because of what we did . . . Did! . . . Here in this yard when Tobias went down. Can you remember what we did? Nothing.

PINKIE. But what could we have done?

WILLIE. Do you know what you've just said? In the space of one minute you've asked me what *can* we do and what *could* we have done. Don't you know what to do at all? Is there nothing you can do except be booted around by life until it looks like your skin was black from the bruises and from nothing else? Guy's right about the thinking I did in there for a week. That's a lot of thinking, but there was a lot to think about. You know one of the ideas I've come out with? The world I live in is the way it is not in spite of me but because of me. You think we're just poor suffering come-to-Jesus-at-the-end-of-it-all black men and that the world's all wrong and against us so what the hell. Well I'm not so sure of that any more. I'm not so sure because I think we helped to make it, the way it is.

WATSON. Are you denying the oppression?

PINKIE. We don't like things the way they are, Willie.

WILLIE. Nobody but a moron would like them. But there's a lot of it we make ourselves and a lot we accept.

PINKIE. Such as?

WILLIE. Such as Tobias's death and a character called Shark. Our handiwork. We've been good customers. Every Friday night in the dot . . . five shillings . . . for a long time. So when a man like Tobias walks in he's out in the cold if he doesn't pay . . . And being a man he wouldn't want to pay. There's nothing that says we must surrender to what we don't like. There's no excuse like saying the world's a big place and I'm just a small little man. My world is as big as I am. Just big enough for me to do something about it. If I can't believe that, there's no point in living. Anyway this doesn't concern any of you and the sooner you leave me alone to solve it my way the better. Well? What are you waiting for . . . or do you want to see how he does it a second time?

[*They all exit except Willie and Guy.*]

WILLIE [*to Guy*]. You'll be late for the show.

GUY. I'm going . . . but not like that. Are you going to wait for him, Willie? [*Pause.*] Willie . . . the world was sweet . . . the world was sweet . . .

WILLIE. It's the way we made it.

GUY [*turning to Willie*]. Then we made it all wrong . . . all wrong and rotten. When I think back to what it was like just a week ago . . . just a week . . . and now. I walked in here with my sax and I found Rebecca. Right there! Taking the washing down. You know who I'm talking about don't you, Willie, or have you forgotten her already?

WILLIE. I won't forget her, Guy.

GUY. Pity you didn't tell her that when she went. It might have saved her a couple of tears . . . even just a couple. Because you do know you said don't you, Willie? You said nothing! Christ, Reb, what happened? What has happened, Willie? No, don't you tell me, don't say a thing. I couldn't take any more from you. Yes, I came home and there she was taking the washing down and talking. She got a little sad about you . . . but she was here! Just a week ago. We even laughed about old Sam. It was here . . . I was here, and Reb, and you were coming home. And it was life . . . tough, hard, but it was life, and I wasn't sorry to be part of it. And then Tobias walked in.

WILLIE. If he hadn't someone else would have and it wouldn't have made any difference.

GUY. Drop the big words and the clever reasons, Willie. Because it was him . . . him . . . Tobias. He walked in here and buggered up everything, buggered up life until I can't recognize it any more. I don't know it . . . I don't know myself . . . I don't know you. You know what Reb said to me this afternoon? She said it was like she went to sleep with one man and woke up to find a stranger beside her in the morning. She meant you. Why did you have to do it? Anything else . . . but why did you have to do that to her, to the two of you? You and Reb was one of the things a fellow could believe in. Whatever else happened you two were there. They could kick me around, Moses could be on the bum but there was always Willie and Reb and they were going places. A good man and a good woman. Now? I can't call you a good man, Willie. I can't believe in what you have done.

WILLIE. Stop trying. There's nothing to believe in.

GUY. What about Willie Seopelo's one-man crusade against crime?

WILLIE. There's no crusade. Just something I had to do, and I'm trying to do it.

GUY. I'm wasting my time arguing with you.

WILLIE. Why must you argue?

GUY. What do you want me to do? Pat you on the back and say 'Good boy'?

WILLIE. What you think you been doing all these years? You, Rebecca, everybody. Good boy, Willie, you passed another exam! Good boy, Willie, you got a rise! Don't you think I'm sick of it? Anyway, that's finished now.

GUY. Are you doing this just because you want to stop that?

WILLIE. No, but it ties up. It was part of everything. It's a long story.

GUY. Too long for two hours.

WILLIE. It's taken me my whole life to live it.

GUY. Your whole life...Willie, the future could be just as long. Why make it two hours?

WILLIE. Because those two hours...Well, I've found something I been looking for for a long time. Peace, Guy, peace. Peace of mind...peace of heart. You know the two old enemies...they're not fighting any more...This is the first time in a long time. But don't think I'm not scared...shit-scared as Shark would say. I'm scared, boy. But there are lots of things to think about and if I try hard enough I can forget...

GUY. Do you want to? Why? Look, Willie...what are you trying to do?...Hide away from what's coming, pretend it's just another Friday night! Shark's coming round...for you...in two hours' time. Are you going to wait? Answer, boy...Because if you can't, start running. [*Pause.*] Are you going to wait?

WILLIE. Yes.

GUY. You're scared, Willie...Run...

WILLIE. No.

GUY. Remember Tobias...they'll do it that way. For the last time, are you going to wait?

WILLIE. It's no use, Guy. I'm scared all right. But then that's human, isn't it? A man's got a right to be scared about a thing like that. Anyway, it's not too bad. I can swallow hard and keep it down and hope it will stay down.

GUY. It's not easy to walk out...you know...just walk out with you standing there.

WILLIE. You'll be late for the show, Guy. It's your big break.

GUY. Help me, Willie...It's hard.

WILLIE. Rebecca. Knock on her door tomorrow. She'll need you. And tonight, play sweet. It's my song. Play sweet, boy.

[*Guy exits and Willie is left alone for a few seconds before Moses, the blind man, enters.*]

MOSES. Is that you, Willie?

WILLIE. Yes.

MOSES. Pinkie's locked the room and gone to the show and I got nowhere to go. So I'll just sit here if it's okay with you, Willie. It won't make no difference...being blind I don't see nothing. He knows that...he knows I can't say nothing in court.

WILLIE. Moses, is it true what they say about blind men, can you hear better than those that see?

MOSES. Yes.

WILLIE. Moses . . .

MOSES. I know, Willie . . . I'll tell you when I hear them coming.

[*Willie moves back to the house. Guy's saxophone music is heard in the background.*]

CURTAIN